Elgar
An Anniversary Portrait

Elgar
An Anniversary Portrait

Introduced by Nicholas Kenyon

continuum

Continuum

The Tower Building 11 York Road London SE1 7NX

80 Maiden Lane Suite 704 New York, NY 10038

www.continuumbooks.com

First published 2007 Reprinted in paperback 2008

British Library Cataloguing-in-Publication Data A catalogue record for this book is available from the British Library.

ISBN 9780826496966 ISBN 9781847065339 (pbk)

Typeset by Interactive Sciences Limited, Gloucestershire Printed and bound by MPG Books Limited, Cornwall

Contents

Introduction

NICHOLAS KENYON

Richard Strauss's famous toast to Edward Elgar in 1902 — 'to the welfare and success of the first English progressivist' — looks startling today. Is not Elgar the last embodiment of a fading Empire, a composer of late romantic music that even for its period was behind the times? That clichéd view has become ever more inadequate over a period when Elgar's music has increasingly been performed and recognized internationally. Yet we all acknowledge that there is something essentially English in Elgar — but what is it? In Elgar we sense a peculiarly British, a (deliberately?) enigmatic combination of conservatism and progressivism, intense introversion and bold extroversion, despair and exuberance. It is easy to see that in the first years of the 20th century, the Wagnerian echoes of *The Dream of Gerontius* and the originality of the *Enigma Variations* must have created a powerful impression on Richard Strauss and others. Was Elgar on the verge of a breakthrough that would have transformed his national music? That did not quite happen. But because it did not happen, something else did.

Elgar was not the only English composer born in the nineteenth century to have travelled abroad and imbibed the effect of the best of continental music, but he was the most successful at internalising the influences. Arthur Sullivan had returned from Leipzig to be hailed as the English Mendelssohn, though his talent found its most distinctive outlet in gentle parody, rather than adventurous development, of the models he studied. Elgar first discovered Wagner, Brahms, Liszt and Berlioz for himself at Covent Garden and Crystal Palace. In 1892–3 he heard all of the Ring cycle, *Parsifal* and

Tristan on visits to Europe, and began to experiment with some of their techniques of harmony and thematic transformation in his not wholly successful choral works of the 1890s. By the time he reached *Gerontius* (a text Dvorak once contemplated setting), he was ready to challenge the heart of the English tradition.

By choosing Cardinal Newman's poem, a Catholic work far outside the tradition of the English establishment oratorio, Elgar immediately broadened the scope of that genre. And by assimilating doubt and uncertainty into his musical picture, Elgar also captured the temper of the times. 'I can no more, for now it comes again/ That sense of ruin which is worse than pain/That masterful negation and collapse/Of all that makes me man'—Elgar's music, rootless and drifting, evokes an feeling of desperation that mirrors Tennyson's *In memoriam* ('I stretch lame hands of faith and grope . . . ') and even Malcolm Arnold's 'Dover Beach' ('The Sea of Faith was once too at the full . . . But now I only hear/Its melancholy, long withdrawing roar . . . ').

Musical England was not ready for *Gerontius*. The performance was famously inadequate and the young Vaughan Williams reported that the tenor sang the part 'like a Stainer anthem, in the correct tenor attitude with one foot slightly withdrawn'. But Elgar's creative life, as documented in this fascinating book of essays, was a continual struggle between the desire for wide, uncritical acceptance and a profound, depressive self-loathing which seems to emerge at the time of his greatest triumphs. And it is surely this emotional tension which both prevented Elgar from becoming a true twentieth-century composer in language and technique, in the way Strauss implied, and yet enabled him to become the composer who more than any other figure expresses truthfully the dichotomies of our country in the early years of the last century.

Just fifty years ago, in a penetrating anniversary essay (*Music and Letters* April 1957), Donald Mitchell started dismissively: 'It is a commonplace that Elgar's reputation has suffered a certain decline. His music, to put it crudely, is a little out of fashion'. You could not write that today: as the essays in this volume charting Elgar's revival and reception make clear, his stock stands higher than ever—revelatory performances and recordings by international interpreters, Solti, Previn, Slatkin, Barenboim, have transformed our understanding of his music (listen to Norrington's recent vibrato-less First Symphony, wonderfully recorded with the SWR Stuttgart Orchestra, reinterpreting the sound of Elgar for the twenty-first century!). And one of the most thrilling musical episodes of recent years (which I had the privilege to be involved in while at BBC Radio 3) has been Anthony Payne's realization of the sketches for Elgar's Third Symphony, first mooted during Radio 3's *Fairest Isle* year in 1995 with an illustrated broadcast talk, and then brought to completion in a studio performance we mounted by Andrew Davis and the BBC Symphony Orchestra on 18 October 1997, in the presence of some of those who had been most sceptical about the possibility of completion, and a Royal Festival Hall account the following spring by the same artists in the BBC's *Sounding the Century* series, hailed as 'a landmark in the history of British music'. That 'new' work has already received well over 100 performances worldwide and has established itself in the repertory, releasing the buried creativity of Elgar's final years.

Mitchell's essay is well worth pursuing, for the central contrast it makes is still absolutely valid, between Elgar as the self-creator of a quintessentially English image (an idea developed in fascinating detail in this volume by David Cannadine), while at the time being more international than all his contemporaries in his musical idiom. And then: 'Elgar's conservative personality—self-imposed as I believe it was—did not mean that he felt less deeply, but rather that the range of his feeling was inhibited: he did not plunge into those new regions of feeling that might have forced his style to widen its scope . . . my guess is that had Elgar liberated himself from a host of protective emotional prohibitions and permitted his tensions to rise to the surface, he might well have responded with some out-of-character music that would have crossed the threshold of the new century in style, not chronology alone.' Absolutely true, and supported by Rosa Burley's observation that Elgar was 'one of the most repressed people it is possible to imagine'. It is perhaps understandable of Mitchell to regret that Elgar did not become more like Mahler, but there is surely one more logical development of his train of thought—that it was precisely *because* Elgar did *not* cross that threshold that he remains such a perfect example of our own (as a nation) emotional inhibition and repressed passion, a passion which bubbles volcanically to the surface in such extraordinarily indirect and ritualized ways—in hymn singing and patriotic displays, in coronations and remembrances, in the laying of flowers for a dead princess. And that is why the true Edward Elgar is equally the Elgar of those agonized, uncertain transitions between the movements of the Cello Concerto, the soloist pulled both ways, not sure where to turn; the Elgar of that terrifying Scherzo of the Second Symphony, almost literally tearing the music apart with passion; the Elgar of the haunting close of the First Symphony's slow movement, with muted brass prophetically pre-echoing the distant conflicts of the century yet to come; and the bumptiously certain Elgar of the first Pomp and Circumstance March, an inevitable feature of every British pageant and every Last Night of the Proms.

A hundred and fifty years since his birth in modest circumstances, we cannot truthfully claim Elgar as our first English progressivist. He has more in common with those great composers, the English madrigalists, or Purcell in his viol fantasias, who achieved great things very late in the day of their chosen forms. But we can surely celebrate him as the first great English internationalist, whose open-ear'd, open-minded, truly humane spirit not only created a uniquely powerful legacy, but opened our window on the wider world, and made possible the towering achievements of British music in the following century.

Nicholas Kenyon has been Director of the BBC Proms since 1996, and becomes Managing Director of the Barbican Centre in October 2007.

Part 1: Elgar the Man

1

Orchestrating His Own Life: Sir Edward Elgar as an Historical Personality[1]

DAVID CANNADINE

Throughout his long years of dogged striving, of eventual triumph, and of elderly decline, Sir Edward Elgar was constantly concerned, not only with being a composer, but also with the fashioning and manipulation of his *image* as a composer. For him, as for his many creative contemporaries across the European continent, there was a varied but limited repertoire of identities that were available for this purpose.[2] The first, which had been briefly outlined by Samuel Johnson in his *Dictionary*, was that of the artist as 'a skilful man': the jobbing practitioner of a serious but essentially prosaic craft, which enabled him to turn an honest penny and even to earn a decent living, but which had nothing to do with genius or greatness or God. It was a matter of calculation rather than of inspiration, of cash instead of cachet, of pennies not prestige. The second identity, exemplified by such painters as Velázquez, Rubens, Van Dyck and Reynolds, was that of the artist as a worldly, courtly, establishment figure: the client of kings, princes and potentates, who was acclaimed, rewarded and honoured by powerful rulers, grateful patrons and, in later times, by an appreciative state. The third was the image of the artist as the isolated, suffering, misunderstood hero, possessed of God-given insights denied lesser, comfortable, conformist mortals—an image originally deriving from the Renaissance, but more recently embodied in the Romantic Movement, and later re-affirmed and re-worked by Ruskin.[3] During the course of his career, Elgar explored and embraced all three of these different (indeed, contradictory) creative identities, but it is only recently that scholars have begun to get the measure of all of *them*—and have thus begun to reach a broader understanding of aspects of *him*.

Elgar's most enduring (and self-indulgent) self-image was that of the martyred genius, pursuing the highest imaginative calling, and writing transcendent music from out of his 'insidest inside' (this was also Alice Elgar's view of her husband), yet all the while suffering for his greatness: inadequately taught, socially disadvantaged, often deeply unhappy, frequently lonely and rejected, constantly thwarted and frustrated, and repeatedly resigned to failure, disillusionment and disappointment. Time and again, Elgar's letters and remarks convey his sense of himself as the victimized, melancholic outsider, who had never received a kindness in his life, who was alienated from his philistine fellow-countrymen, who was convinced that God was against great art, whose best work was denied a decent hearing, whose whole existence had been wasted, who loathed and scorned the world, who sometimes seemed on the verge of complete mental breakdown, and who in his late, barren, neglected years, when he had outlived his own inspiration, even came to 'hate' music itself.[4] To be sure, there were aspects and episodes of Elgar's life which corroborated this tortured self-image: among them the long struggle out of provincial obscurity, the failed first performances of *The Dream of Gerontius* and the Second Symphony, the decline of his creative output after 1911, and the death of his wife nine years later. And Elgar further embellished this romantic identity with the myths and enigmas he cultivated about himself and his friends: the child by the River Severn, 'longing for something very great'; the concealed identities of those he put in his music or to whom he dedicated it; his famous but unknown last words; and so on.[5] Moreover, it is this Elgar—inspired yet desolate, who was different from ordinary, lesser mortals; the music maker, the seer of visions, and the dreamer of dreams—who inhabits the early biographies by Basil Maine, Percy M. Young and Diana McVeagh, and also the more recent works by Michael Kennedy, Jerrold Northrop Moore and Michael de-la-Noy.[6]

This was Elgar as he wanted to be seen during his own lifetime, and it is a measure of his success in managing this essentially romantic, highly selective, and self-regarding self-image that so much of the writing about him since his death has uncritically accepted it. Yet there also co-existed a second and very different Elgar: the socially ambitious self-promoter, obsessed with fame and titles and royalty, who was resolved to 'conquer' the great world, and who eventually did so with remarkable success.[7] This was the man who married for money (£100 a year) and status at least as much as for love and reassurance; who sought and cultivated aristocratic and plutocratic friends to promote his music and his cause; who did all he could to ingratiate himself at the courts of Queen Victoria, King Edward VII and King George V; who never refused an honour and who was disappointed not to receive more of them; and who hoped 'some day to do a great work—a sort of national thing that my fellow Englishmen might take to themselves and love'.[8] This was also the man who donned evening dress or court dress or academic dress whenever possible; who delighted in wearing his stars and ribbons and collars and medals; and who cultivated the demeanour of a retired colonel or a country squire. Here was a very different Elgar: gruff, no-nonsense, conformist, down-to-earth, well-connected—the very antithesis of the tortured outsider he also liked to be and to play. From this perspective, it is clear that Elgar was determined to disprove one of the nineteenth century's conventional wisdoms, namely that it was impossible for anyone to be both an artist and a gentleman at the same time. He wanted to be both, and in that deliberate and sustained endeavour he undoubtedly succeeded.[9]

Those among Elgar's biographers who accept his self-pitying yet self-serving self-image at face value tend to dismiss his affectations of gentility and his thirst for honours as the things he did primarily to please his wife, or as the grudging recognition by the state and his sovereign to which his transcendent talents undoubtedly entitled him. But these objectives were clearly much more important to him than that: he devoted a great deal of time and effort to attaining and achieving them, and it cannot always have been easy for Elgar to sustain these two contrasted and inconsistent personae—the spurned outsider and the acclaimed insider—throughout his professional life; no wonder, despite his ambition, tenacity and determination, he often seemed so uncertain and unsure of himself.[10] Yet there was also a third Elgar, who has only recently begun to come into focus: not so much the tradesman who always resented and regretted his humble social origins, but the man of business in the tradition of Dickens and Trollope, who understood the close relationship between creativity and cash, productivity and revenue, and who was more successful at making money than he was inclined to let on.[11] 'You know', he told his friend August Jaeger in 1898, 'that £.s.d. is a serious matter to me', and music was the means of making it. Between 1897 and 1909, Elgar's income grew tenfold, from £200 to £2,000, the latter being the equivalent of £100,000 in today's values. But once the money began to come in from other sources, the music-making ceased: during the 1920s, the proceeds from the sale of Severn House in London, the inheritance from his late wife, and the retainer he was paid by The Gramophone Company meant there was no financial imperative to compose, and so he stopped composing. Indeed, it was only when the money began to run out, during the early 1930s, that Elgar went seriously back to work. As an Australian critic had noted as early as 1903, 'Dr Elgar is not only a musician of undoubted talent, but also a smart businessman.'[12]

These three different Elgars—the rejected genius, the rewarded courtier, and the shrewd man of money—were the composer's own variations on the standard templates of artistic self-fashioning and self-presentation that were available during his lifetime; they are fully documented in his correspondence and in the reminiscences of his friends and contemporaries, and any future biography of Elgar should do equal justice to each of them, explaining how he handled their many contradictions and finessed their inherent inconsistencies. But if we are to make better sense of Elgar as an historical personality, one hundred and fifty years since his birth, then we also need to get some additional distance on him, by setting and seeing his life more explicitly in the context of when lived, where he worked, and what he did.[13] To that end, this essay will sketch out Elgar's place in his time-bound and place-specific world, by examining it at three levels, which will become 'wider still and wider', as they extend from locality, via nation, to empire. The essential starting place is Worcester and the Severn Valley, for Elgar was in many ways a recognizable product of the city's lower-middle class and of the region's prevailing conservative culture. But he was determined to break out, to make himself a national figure, and to be honoured and recognized as such, and the second section explores the obstacles he encountered, and the opportunities he exploited, as he travelled the path to becoming Britain's unofficial (and, latterly, official) laureate composer. In the light of these local and national considerations, the third part of this study will re-consider Elgar's work as an imperial composer, and suggest that when it came to the greater world beyond Britain, his first-hand experience and creative engagement were not so much with the British Empire (as was the case with Kipling and Lutyens), but with Europe, and especially with Germany.

I

Elgar's local roots are exceptionally important in understanding him, not only geographically, sociologically and politically, but also mythologically, for his own version of his upbringing was highly selective, and his biographers have tended to follow him in placing undue stress on the disadvantages he had to overcome, rather than the considerable advantages he enjoyed (and exploited). In one guise, to be sure, Elgar was immensely proud of his Worcester origins: he lived there until his marriage in 1889, he remained abidingly loyal to the city thereafter and visited the place regularly, and he spent the last five years of his life there.[14] But he was also extremely sensitive to metropolitan accusations that he was a provincial, and he always resented the fact that he had been compelled to spend the first forty years of his life working as a 'local musician' in a distant backwater, eking out a living by teaching the violin and conducting the band in the nearby lunatic asylum.[15] Yet this is scarcely the whole truth of things. During the 1850s, the decade when Elgar was born, towns like Worcester, York, Exeter and Lincoln remained more typical of urban England than cities such as Leeds, Liverpool, Manchester or Birmingham: the old world of Barchester still had the edge over the new world of

Coketown.[16] Moreover, Worcester itself was a flourishing county town and a regional metropolis: its population expanded from 13,000 to 46,000 across the nineteenth century, it provided financial and marketing services for the surrounding agricultural district, and its locally based industries included porcelain and glove-making. It was also a major transport hub: the Severn was the longest navigable river in Great Britain; the Worcester and Birmingham Canal had opened in 1815; and railways would eventually link the city to London, Bristol and Birmingham in one direction, and to Ludlow, Hereford, the north-west and South Wales in another. At least in terms of trains, Worcester was an easy town to get out of during Elgar's time.[17]

Nevertheless, Elgar always insisted that he had been doubly disadvantaged at birth, for he was not merely a provincial, but a lower-middle-class provincial whose family were *in trade*: his father was a piano-tuner who owned a music shop in Worcester, and who entered by the back door when he visited the nearby big houses to adjust the instruments of the local gentry. Although he remained devoted to his relatives, this abiding sense of social inferiority seems to have left Elgar with a life-long chip on his shoulder.[18] Yet once again, he retrospectively exaggerated the obstacles in his way: by the standards of the time, he had received a relatively good education, remaining at school until the age of fourteen; his parents were respectable and rich enough to keep three servants; and by the 1890s the annual turnover of Elgar Brothers was in the region of £100,000 in today's values. He was neither born nor brought up in philistine poverty.[19] Elgar was also lucky in belonging to the traditional lower-middle class of traders, shopkeepers and clerks which inhabited cathedral cities and county towns, rather than to the new, more anonymous, petty bourgeoisie of clerks, managers and white-collar workers which was expanding rapidly in London and in the industrial midlands and the north of England. True to their local background and social position, the Elgar family took a fiercely individualistic view of life, they were careful with their money, they had no time for the collective solidarities of class, they disliked and distrusted blue-collar manual workers, they were strongly status-conscious, they were eager to improve themselves and to rise in the world, and they were deeply respectful of the established order of things. The young Edward Elgar imbibed these views as a boy, they remained with him all his life, and together with his particular Worcester background, they tell us much about him: he was the recognizable product of a conservative class in a conservative city.[20]

Elgar's early years must rank as one of the fullest lower-middle-class lives ever documented, and for all his regret at what he came to regard as Worcester's parochial limitations, his boyhood and adolescence were, in social and cultural terms, both rich and rewarding. As a precocious and versatile instrumentalist, he participated fully in the vigorous associational life of the city which, thanks to the great cathedral in its midst, was centred on music-making. From the age of fifteen he deputized for his father as organist at St George's Church, he joined the 'instrumental nights' at the local Glee Club, he was 'Leader and Instructor' for the Amateur Instrumental Society, and he eventually formed his own woodwind quintet. One of his collaborators in this latter enterprise was Hubert Aloysius Leicester, a school friend and close contemporary, to whom he would remain close for more than seventy years. Unlike Elgar, Leicester would spend his whole life in the city, where he worked as an accountant; he was five times Mayor of Worcester, in 1905, and again from 1911 to 1916; and he would be knighted in 1939, the last year of his life. Elgar was delighted with his friend, for so 'splendidly upholding the honour of our town', and in 1908 dedicated the second suite of *The Wand of Youth* to him.[21] Like similar figures elsewhere (for example Gurney Benham in Colchester), Hubert Leicester was also a local historian and antiquarian of note, and one of his books, *Forgotten Worcester*, was published in 1930, with a preface by Elgar, which recalled their shared schoolboy interest in such icons and emblems of hierarchy as 'mayors, corporations, Lord Lieutenants and clergy'.[22]

As these activities and observations make plain, the generation to which Leicester and Elgar belonged lived out their lives against a vivid backdrop of burgeoning civic consciousness, civic pride and civic pageantry, which flourished across the length and breadth of urban England, mimicking and paralleling the efflorescence of royal ceremonial and imperial display in London itself.[23] During his lifetime, Elgar participated in many such occasions in Worcester, and as his fame grew, he was, increasingly, at the centre of them. One of his earliest works, *Sursum Corda*, was a ceremonial piece for brass, organ and strings, composed to welcome the Duke of York on a visit to the city in 1894. Eleven years later, during Hubert Leicester's first term as Mayor, Elgar was given the Freedom of the City of Worcester, and processed through the town resplendent in his robes as a Doctor of Music of Yale University, doffing his cap to his father, who looked down from a window above the family shop. In 1914, the landscape painter, Benjamin Leader, was similarly honoured, and at the ensuing civic banquet, Elgar proposed the toast to 'The Faithful City and her sons'. In 1923, a portrait of Elgar by Sir Philip Burne-Jones was hung in Worcester Guildhall; in the following year he spoke when the Freedom of the City was conferred upon the long-serving Town Clerk; and when Hubert Leicester himself was made a Freeman in 1932, Elgar was there again (Leicester's own portrait would be unveiled in the Guildhall soon after). 'My thoughts', Elgar remarked on one of these occasions, 'are always with the old place, its old institutions, its poetry and romance.'[24] Nor was Elgar's delight in municipal flummery confined to his native city: in 1905, he was invited to serve as Mayor of Hereford (he resided in the city from 1904 to 1911, but wisely refused the request), and in 1927 he composed a civic fanfare for the Corporation.

Worcester was also important to Elgar in another way, for its military history was both lengthy and significant, and it was still being made during his own lifetime. From the eleventh to the fifteenth centuries, the city had been the base from which successive English kings had launched their attacks on Wales and the Marches; between 1642 and 1646 Worcester had stubbornly and loyally supported Charles I, surrendering only at the very end of the Civil War; and the local Worcestershire Regiment could trace its history continuously back to the early eighteenth century, with Ramillies as its earliest battle honour. Thereafter, the Worcesters fought in the Revolutionary and Napoleonic Wars, in India during the 1830s, and in South Africa during the Boer War.[25] It was, then, difficult to avoid the presence of the military in Worcester: the façade of the Guildhall was brilliantly decorated with trophies and garlands, there were regimental flags and monuments in the

cathedral, and soldiers' parades were a regular feature of city life.
Much of Elgar's delight in military marches, and in what he later
described (quoting Shakespeare's *Othello*) as the 'pride, pomp and
circumstance of glorious war' may be ascribed to his childhood
memories of watching the Queen's troops passing by. On more than
one occasion, he suggested that there was 'some of the soldier
instinct in me', and that had he not been a musician he would have
joined the army; and many observers noted (and some later
criticized) Elgar's military dress and demeanour. 'I like to look on
the composer's vocation', he observed in an interview discussing his
first two *Pomp and Circumstance* marches, 'as the old troubadours
or bards did. In those days it was no disgrace for a man to be turned
on to step in front of an army and inspire them with a song.'[26]

All his life, Elgar was fascinated by robes and maces, genealogy
and heraldry, uniforms and coats of arms, swords and longbows,
banners and flags, displays and processions, and it is more than just
coincidence that his great years of creativity coincided with one of
the most ornamental—or, to borrow his own word, *nobilmente*
—phases of British civic and military life. But these were merely the
accoutrements and outward expression of the ancient ideal of
chivalry, which was vigorously revived during the nineteenth
century; and like others of his class with aspirations to gentility,
Elgar embraced it eagerly and enthusiastically, and not just in his
Pomp and Circumstance marches. Among his earlier works, *Froissart*, *The Black Knight*, *King Olaf*, *The Banner of St George* and
Caractacus had all been drawn from historical and romantic tales,
centred around individual heroism and knight-errantry, and they
were dominated by figures who 'lifted their lances on high'. The
overture *Cockaigne* contains a section depicting a military procession passing along the streets of London. English music, Elgar later
insisted, in the lectures he delivered at the University of Birmingham, should be 'broad, noble, chivalrous, healthy and out-of-doors', his words echoing *The Broad Stone of Honour* by Sir
Kenelm Digby, which was one of the founding texts of the chivalric
revival.[27] At the other end of his creative career, the overture
Falstaff was a more elegiac treatment of the chivalric ideal; when he
composed *The Spirit of England* during the First World War, it was
dedicated to 'the memory of our glorious men, with a special

thought for the Worcesters'; and in 1923 he produced the incidental music for *Arthur*, a play by Laurence Binyon, which re-told the classic tale of knightly gallantry, courtly intrigue and ultimate betrayal.

For all his relatively humble social origins, Worcester thus provided Elgar with ample music and friendship, and also with abundant civic pageantry and martial splendour. All this reinforced that 'inner core of conservatism' which characterized the lower-middle class into which he had been born, so it is scarcely surprising that he became a staunch and life-long Tory. (The politics of the artist, Stephen Spender once observed, were those of the un-political: but this was emphatically not true in Elgar's case.)[28] As such he found the parliamentary politics of his native city increasingly congenial. For half a century following the Great Reform Act, Worcester had generally returned two Liberal MPs, but in 1885 it was made a single-member constituency, and thereafter it was a safe Tory seat. For the next 21 years, it was represented by George Allsopp, whose father, a brewer with local connections, would be ennobled in 1886 as Lord Hindlip. (One of George's brothers, the Hon. Alfred Allsopp, also served as Mayor of Worcester in 1892, in 1894, and again in 1909.) Along with his friend Hubert Leicester, who wrote political pamphlets under the pseudonym 'Eusebius', Elgar was an active force in Worcester politics, campaigning for the Conservatives in successive general elections, and this brought him into personal contact with the Allsopp dynasty. In part perhaps because of their beer and largesse, Worcester was widely regarded as a deeply corrupt constituency, where voters of 'the needy and loafing class', and also of 'working men in regular employment', were prepared to sell their votes 'for drink or money'. As a result, the Tories held on to the seat in 1906, against the prevailing Liberal landslide; but the victor was unseated on petition, and Elgar himself considered standing in the Conservative interest, urging Hubert Leicester to find out 'how the land lies'. Had he contested it at the ensuing by-election, he would surely have been elected, but he wisely declined.[29]

As a county town with a conservative political culture, which was the centre of a large agricultural region, the citizens of Worcester had always 'shown a high degree of deference to their social superiors in the countryside', and this was an attitude shared by Elgar's father, who had relied for some of his business on noble and gentry patronage.[30] For Worcester was an ordered, layered county, with its social hierarchy extending from peers and notables such as Lords Beauchamp, Coventry, Lyttelton, Foley and Sandys, via the baronetcy, gentry and clergy, to the yeoman farmers and agricultural labourers at the base. There were few great grandees, or massive Whig palaces, or vast estates: Elgar's Worcester might resemble Trollope's Barchester in some ways, but there was no Duke of Omnium residing in the vicinity, and the countryside was dominated by the middling landowners and the greater gentry, who were often Tory in politics and conservative in culture.[31] The neighbouring counties of Hereford, Gloucester and Shropshire, all of which drained into the River Severn, were very similar in structure and tone. There were no great industrial cities, there were few great grandees (the Duke of Beaufort at Badminton being the exception who proved the rule), and the occupants of the manor houses and rural rectories tended to share the parochial outlook of their Worcestershire neighbours.[32] Indeed, it was the adjacent Tory-gentry world of Gloucestershire that produced Elgar's friend and patron, Sir Hubert Parry, descended from a line of Severn-side squires who lived at Highnam Court. But whereas Parry rejected the 'sterile' culture and values of the world into which he had been born, and became a lifelong Liberal, Elgar embraced whole-heartedly the Tory culture and traditional values of the world to which he aspired.[33]

He carved out two determined and successful routes into it, and they were, unsurprisingly, via his music and via his marriage. As a cathedral city, Worcester was not only a major musical metropolis in its own right, but it was also linked to Hereford and Gloucester via the Three Choirs Festival, which dated back to the early eighteenth century, and which was held by rotation in each city in late summer. Elgar's father played in the Three Choirs Orchestra, and the son duly followed suit, beginning in 1878. This brought him into immediate contact with the symphonies and the oratorios of the contemporary musical scene (Dvořák conducted his Sixth Symphony at Worcester in 1884, when Elgar was playing in the first violins). It also enabled him to make lifelong friendships with the three cathedral organists: Ivor Atkins at Worcester, Alfred Herbert Brewer at Gloucester, and G. R. Sinclair at Hereford. And there were some important early commissions: a short orchestral work for 1889; *The Light of Life*, an oratorio, for 1896; and a *Te Deum* and *Benedictus* for the following year.[34] Meanwhile, in 1889 Elgar had married Alice Roberts, to whom he had been giving lessons in piano accompaniment. Her father, Major General Sir Henry Roberts, had enjoyed a distinguished career as an army officer in the East India Company, had been made a Knight Commander of the Order of the Bath for his efforts during the Indian Mutiny, and had subsequently set himself up as a country gentleman at Hazeldine House, near Redmarley d'Abitot, on the Worcestershire-Gloucestershire border. By marrying Alice Roberts, Elgar was making a most advantageous match: for she not only brought (some) money into their marriage, but also social connections. She may have married 'down', and some of her relatives disowned her as a result, but Elgar had emphatically married 'up', and he was now seriously launched into county society. Henceforward, the houses of the Severn-side nobility and gentry were open to both of them and, unlike William Elgar, his son Edward entered them through the front door rather than via the tradesman's entrance at the back.[35]

From this formative and localist perspective, by turns constraining yet full of the promise and opportunities that he eagerly sought to seize, the culmination of this first phase of Elgar's life was the composition of the *Enigma Variations*, which took place between 1898 and 1899. One way of seeing that work is as the most fully formed, deeply felt and considered expression of his romantic self-image as the creative artist: preoccupied with his solitary, inner life, but also well aware of the sustaining importance of the 'Friends Pictured Within'.[36] Yet another way of seeing it is as a rare and remarkable display of what might be termed musical sociology: for in their mixture of autobiography and biography, the *Variations* are also an account of the local networks and individual connections, spreading out from Worcester to the surrounding countryside and counties beyond, that Elgar, assisted by his wife, had succeeded in establishing during the preceding decade. Hence his homage to (among others) William Meath Baker, a country squire resident at

Hasfield Court near Gloucester; to Arthur Troyte Griffith, a Malvern architect; to Dr Sinclair, the organist of Hereford Cathedral; and to Lady Mary Lygon of Madresfield, whose brother, Lord Beauchamp, had been Mayor of Worcester in 1895–96, following Alfred Allsopp. Thus regarded, the *Variations* were a portrait gallery and prosopography of the gentrified, conservative culture of Severn-side; but as music, they were anything but derivative, for they were highly original in both their form and construction. Nor was this their only paradox: for in thus celebrating the city and the shires he had finally conquered, Elgar was also creating for himself the means of escaping from them to the broader national stage (and to the broader national recognition) that he had always craved.[37]

II

But while it was one thing for Elgar, with the help of his wife, to conquer Worcestershire, Herefordshire, Gloucestershire and Shropshire by the close of the nineteenth century, it was quite another for him, and for them, to triumph in London and to subjugate the nation at the beginning of the twentieth. To be sure, the 1850s, the decade of his birth, had witnessed unprecedented efforts at improving geographical mobility in Britain, and also an unprecedented discussion (and proclamation) of social mobility. The creation of a national railway network made it easier and cheaper than ever before to journey from the provinces to London, as evidenced by the huge working-class crowds who made the trip to visit the Great Exhibition in 1851. In the previous year, Lord Palmerston had saluted Britain for being a nation where, uniquely, 'each individual of each class is constantly trying to raise himself in the social scale, not by violence and illegality, but by persevering good conduct.'[38] In 1856, the National Portrait Gallery was founded, and one of its animating purposes was to display the likenesses of eminent Britons, in the hope that those visitors born in humbler circumstances might be inspired to emulate their iconic achievements. And three years later, Samuel Smiles published his famous panegyric on self-improvement and self-advancement, which he entitled *Self-Help*. Yet during the 1850s, and for the remainder of the nineteenth century, there was always a large gap in Britain between such aspiration and the actuality, especially for those towards the bottom end of the social scale. In the same year that *Self-Help* appeared, *The Times* offered a very different perspective: 'ninety-nine people in a hundred', it observed, more realistically, 'cannot "get on" in life, but are tied by birth, education or circumstances to a lower position, where they must stay.'[39]

All his life, Elgar shared this pessimistic sociological view: despite his 'persevering good conduct', it was one of his constant complaints that he had not found it easy to 'get on'. As someone who had been born not only lower-middle class, but also Roman Catholic, he was convinced that 'post after post' had been denied him on the grounds of his religion, and one of the many reasons given for the unenthusiastic response to the first performance of *Gerontius* in nonconformist Birmingham was that the work 'stank of incense'.[40] As a self-taught and self-made man, he felt shut out of the academic world of the British musical establishment, and he was never at ease in colleges or with professors: witness his disastrous lectures delivered at the University of Birmingham (that city again!) and also his long-running feud with Charles Villiers Stanford. By the time Elgar reached his twenties and thirties, the countryside was enduring a protracted agricultural depression, accompanied by widespread depopulation: as such it was increasingly marginalized from mainstream British life in a way that had not been true when he had been growing up. It was to the great industrial cities, and to the even greater world metropolis of London, that the balance of political, social and cultural power had now shifted, but Elgar was not at ease to the north or south-east of Worcester. He did not like the factories or the workers to be found in Leeds, Liverpool, Manchester or Sheffield (let alone Birmingham), and he did not 'belong' to their choral societies and music festivals in the way that he felt at home in Worcester, Hereford and Gloucester.[41] Nor was London initially any more welcoming: after marrying Alice Roberts in 1889, the couple had settled down in the capital, hoping Edward's talents might be recognized and his career advanced. But the venture was a humiliating failure, and after two lean years, the Elgars returned to Worcestershire to lick their wounds, and they did not return to London to live until 1912.

Yet as with his constant complaints about the parochialism and limitations of his early life in lower-middle-class Worcester, Elgar also protested too much about the national obstacles he later faced. By the close of the nineteenth century, English Roman Catholics were increasingly tolerated and assimilated into public life: unlike their pro-Home Rule Irish counterparts, they tended (as with Elgar himself) to be Unionist and to vote Tory, and one of them, the Duke of Norfolk, sat in Lord Salisbury's Conservative cabinet as Paymaster General.[42] Elgar may have been determinedly 'buttoned up' in the presence of professors, and when lecturing on university campuses, but Stanford had vigorously supported Elgar during the early stages of his career, he would eventually receive seven honorary doctorates from universities in Britain and the United States, and he was made a member of many European Academies. By the same token, Elgar's Worcestershire might seem increasingly marginal to the nation's political, social and cultural life by the late nineteenth century, but in the early 1900s, three members of Balfour's Conservative cabinet were from local families or represented local constituencies: Lord Windsor, Alfred Lyttelton and Austen Chamberlain.[43] And although Elgar was ill at ease in the music festivals of the great midland and northern cities, they were a regular source of patronage for some of his major commissions and the setting for some of his most significant first performances: among them *King Olaf* at Hanley, North Staffordshire, in 1897, *Caractacus* at Leeds in 1898, *Gerontius* at Birmingham in 1900, the *Coronation Ode* at Sheffield in 1902, and *The Apostles* and *The Kingdom* at Birmingham in 1903 and 1906, respectively. As for London, Elgar's first assault on the metropolis was undeniably premature, for he had an insufficient body of work behind him; but however deep his humiliation, this did not prevent him from composing a memorable evocation of the city in his overture *Cockaigne* (1901), which was subtitled *In London Town*.

Moreover, Elgar clearly learned from his first London rebuff, when he had mistakenly launched himself upon the great city with inadequate connections and few major works to his credit, for while strengthening his local contacts during the 1890s, he also began, through them, to reach out beyond his Severn-side friends to create a broader, national network of benefactors and potential patrons. In this endeavour he achieved considerable success, especially as the great compositions began to flow, from the *Enigma Variations* onwards, and Elgar became a name to conjure with and he himself a man to know. Some of his closest comrades were, unsurprisingly, musicians or those connected with the performing arts: most famously the publisher August Jaeger ('Nimrod' in the *Enigma Variations*), and Hans Richter (who conducted the premieres of *Enigma*, *Gerontius* and the First Symphony). Some were rich businessmen and plutocrats, including Alfred Rodewald (to whom Elgar dedicated his first *Pomp and Circumstance* march), the financier Sir Edgar Speyer (who introduced Elgar to Richard Strauss), and the banker Frank Schuster (who would leave Elgar £7,000 in his will). Others were aristocrats whose interests in the arts transcended any party political affiliation: the (Liberal) Marquess of Northampton, who was an amateur musician and a major landowner in the neighbouring county of Warwickshire; Lady Maud Warrender, a daughter of the Earl of Shaftesbury and an in-law of the Allsopps, who was a fine amateur singer; Lord Edmund Talbot, a Catholic peer and relative of the Duke of Norfolk, whom the Elgars met at a Sheffield Music Festival; and Lady Alice Stuart-Wortley, the daughter of the painter Millais and the wife of Lord Stuart of Wortley, who as 'Windflower' became a lifelong friend and whose spirit would eventually be enshrined in Elgar's Violin Concerto.

This is not to suggest that all of Elgar's friendships were cynically inaugurated and exclusively calculated with his eye to the main chance. But he came from a class that has rightly been described as being particularly 'susceptible to personal co-optation and patronage', and there can be no doubt that Elgar's individual preferences and his professional ambitions often converged. Assisted and encouraged by his wife, he became a tireless and accomplished networker, both locally and nationally, and he was equally resourceful and energetic when it came to ingratiating himself with the British monarchy. As a lower-middle-class Tory, Elgar was an instinctive loyalist and royalist, and Worcester's much-vaunted faithfulness to successive sovereigns was well embodied in the statues of Charles I, Charles II and Queen Anne which adorned the Guildhall.[44] But once again, there were personal connections for him to explore and exploit. Among his many county clients, Elgar's father had been the piano tuner to Queen Adelaide, the widow of King William IV, after she had taken up residence at nearby Witley Court, while Walter Parratt, who was later knighted and appointed the Master of the King's Musick, had been the organist at Great Witley Church from 1861 to 1868. And Elgar also had courtly connections of his own: Lady Mary Lygon of Madresfield, whom he immortalized in the *Enigma Variations*, was a Lady-in-Waiting to the Duchess of York (the future Queen Mary) as, subsequently, was her sister, Lady Margaret Lygon. Their brother, the seventh Earl Beauchamp, was not only Mayor of Worcester but was also a minor Liberal politician, in which capacity he served as Lord Steward of the Household from 1907 to 1910, and he carried the Sword of State at the coronation of George V. In addition, George Allsopp, the one-time Conservative MP for Worcester, was married to a sister of the ninth Earl of Shaftesbury, and in a later generation Shaftesbury, too, would be Lord Steward of the Household, from 1922 to 1936.

These were potentially powerful and important royal connections, and after his initial rebuff in London, Elgar adopted a more considered and calculating approach to conquering the metropolis, not so much by himself as via the monarchy, and to this end he lobbied his courtly friends in high places persistently, vigorously —and successfully—from the late 1890s. It was a propitious time to do so, for a Crown that was in the process of aggrandizing itself ceremonially was also increasingly in need of musical accompaniment.[45] Once again, his initial efforts were disappointing, for Queen Victoria refused to accept the dedication of the *Imperial March* which Elgar had composed to celebrate her Diamond Jubilee in 1897 and which in form and style was the precursor of his later 'pomp and circumstance' works. But thanks to enlisting the help of Sir Walter Parratt and Lady Mary Lygon, he prevailed the second time around, as Victoria accepted the dedication of *Caractacus* a year later, and this was followed by the dedication of the part-song 'To Her Beneath Whose Steadfast Star'. As a result, Elgar was now welcomed to the royal court, and soon after there was a command performance of his works at Windsor Castle. But this success with the Queen-Empress was merely the beginning, for the next sovereign, King Edward VII, adored the great tune in the first *Pomp and Circumstance* march, and with the words added by A. C. Benson it formed the climax of the *Coronation Ode* which Elgar composed in 1902, along with a special coronation hymn, 'O Mightiest of the Mighty'. In the following year, King Edward and Queen Alexandra attended the three-day Elgar festival held at Covent Garden, and Elgar believed that the 'dear sweet King-Man' had taken a 'great fancy' to him and his music.[46] Quite by coincidence, Edward VII's reign coincided with an unprecedented interest in royal ceremonial and also with Elgar's golden period of creativity and fame, and in 1911 he dedicated his Second Symphony to the late king's memory.

By now, Elgar had established himself as (among other things) the court composer par excellence, and to help inaugurate the new reign of King George V, he produced a *Coronation March*; he composed the offertory for chorus and orchestra, 'O hearken thou' that was sung at the service in Westminster Abbey; and a pencil portrait of him was commissioned and hung at Windsor Castle at about this time. To be sure, Elgar thought the new king and queen 'incapable of appreciating anything artistic' (how did this distinguish them from their immediate predecessors?) and their court 'irredeemably vulgar' (ditto), and he refused to contribute to Queen Mary's dolls house scheme. But he had no intention of abandoning his hard-won royal standing and across the ensuing years he dutifully composed some minor works: the setting of an ode by John Masefield in memory of Queen Alexandra, music for the king's recovery from illness, and the Nursery Suite dedicated to the Duchess of York, Princess Elizabeth and Princess Margaret Rose.[47] Part cause, part consequence of these later efforts was that in 1924, on the death of Sir Walter Parratt, Elgar was appointed Master of the King's Musick. There were calls for the abolition of the post altogether, but Elgar lobbied shamelessly and successfully not only that the office should be retained, but also that he should be given it. In this capacity, he became even more of a courtier, advising about such matters as the future of a possible English opera company, the correct version of the National Anthem to be played on the BBC, the musical events it was appropriate for members of the royal family to attend, and so on. And Elgar also intervened to press for honours to be awarded his fellow-composers, including a knighthood for Granville Bantock in 1930 and the Companion of Honour for Delius at almost the end of his life.

By then, Elgar knew a great deal about the nation's honours system, since he himself had become increasingly festooned with badges and sashes and stars. This was partly a matter of supply: for Elgar lived in, and was the active beneficiary of, an era of almost unprecedented honorific proliferation and aggrandizement, the like of which had not been seen in Britain since the Revolutionary and Napoleonic Wars a century before. Between the last years of Queen Victoria and the early years of King George V, new orders of chivalry were invented at what in retrospect seems an almost frenzied pace, among them the Royal Victorian Order, the Order of Merit, the Order of the British Empire and the Order of Companions of Honour. At the same time, knighthoods and peerages were given out more extravagantly than any period since the late eighteenth century, and to a far wider social group than previously. And in the era of Lloyd George and Maundy Gregory, it was widely (and truthfully) rumoured that some politicians were selling knighthoods and peerages for cash.[48] But even though more honours were available, and for more people than ever before, Elgar's eventual accumulation was entirely unprecedented for a British composer. He was knighted at the suggestion of the Conservative Prime Minister, Arthur Balfour, in 1904, and although he could not have expected any further recognition from the Liberal governments of 1905–16, he was awarded the Order of Merit by George V at the time of his Coronation in 1911. (The new sovereign, or at least his advisors, were clearly not as philistine as Elgar thought.) As such, Elgar was the first composer to be so recognized, he far outstripped such predecessors, contemporaries and rivals as Sullivan, Parry or Stanford, and in the following year he finally established himself in London, in opulent comfort at Severn House in Hampstead, where he would delight in aping 'royal state'.[49]

It has often been argued that Elgar accepted his knighthood and his OM not for himself but to give pleasure to his wife: in part because he (rightly) felt he owed her a great deal for her unwavering belief in his genius; and also because she was very conscious of having married a man of lowlier social status than might have been expected of the daughter of a Major General and a Knight Commander of the Order of the Bath. As their daughter Carice Elgar revealingly put it in 1904, 'I am so glad for mother's sake that father has been knighted. You see—it puts her back where she was.' It has also been alleged that Elgar buried all his baubles with Lady Elgar on her death in 1920 because he believed that without her he would never have achieved them.[50] But providing honorific reassurance for his wife and expressing his gratitude to her were not his only motivations. For as befitted a self-confessed lover of hierarchy, history and pageantry, who was a tireless self-promoter and eager for public recognition, Elgar was also keenly interested in such matters himself: during his lifetime there was determined honorific demand as well as abundant honorific supply. He was fascinated by tracking his own rise in the formal order of precedence as his honours mounted up; he was delighted that his Order of Merit outranked anything that his father-in-law (only a KCB) or Lord Beauchamp (a mere Knight Commander of the Order of St Michael and St George) had been awarded; and in 1913 he stormed out of the Royal Academy banquet because 'they had omitted my OM and put me with a crowd of nobodies in the lowliest place of all—the bottom table'.[51]

In any case, the most emphatic proof that Elgar did not accept honours just to give pleasure to his wife lies in the fact that he garnered more of them after her death than he had done during the years when she had been alive. In 1928 he was made a Knight Commander of the Royal Victorian Order, an honour in the personal gift of the sovereign and in appreciation of his work as Master of the King's Musick. He described it in one letter as 'wretched' and 'awful', but he protested altogether too much, and in 1933 he was happily advanced to the highest rank of Knight Grand Cross. No composer since Elgar's time has thus been recognized by royalty and during these fallow years as a composer he clearly owed these honours to his courtly connections rather than to any new work he was undertaking. But none of this satisfied him, for throughout the post-war period he hankered after a peerage. 'I fear it is hopeless,' he told Lady Stuart of Wortley, in importunately pessimistic vein, 'but it would please me.' In 1924 and again in 1927 he urged his friends to talk to Lord Beauchamp and to Lord Shaftesbury, in the hope that they might be able to deliver.[52] Eventually, in 1931, he was given a baronetcy and became Sir Edward Elgar of Broadheath, in homage to his Worcestershire birthplace. It was, indeed, a hereditary honour; but since he had no son, the title died with him; and in any case, it was not the much-wanted peerage. Be that as it may, Elgar's supposed indifference to honours is scarcely borne out by the evidence. Unlike Vaughan Williams, who later refused all honours that might have put him under an obligation to anyone in authority, Elgar accepted everything that was going, lobbied hard via his friends for them, and plainly wanted more.[53]

It is, then, clear that Elgar was as fully at home in an era of royal and honorific aggrandizement as he was in the era of municipal ceremonial and civic ornamentalism, and that he made his way in both worlds by a determined combination of music and manoeuvring, of creativity and calculation. Indeed, so successful was Elgar in establishing himself as *the* national composer of his day, who was both laureate and lauded, that the position he created, and the recognition that went with it, both became institutionalized in Britain in the years since his death. There have been no further proposals to abolish the post of Master of the King's Musick, and although there have never been fixed 'slots' in the Order of Merit assigned to particular fields of academic or creative endeavour, it has been a generally accepted convention since Elgar's time that one of its members ought to be a composer. Accordingly, the OM was bestowed upon Vaughan Williams (the only honour he would accept) soon after Elgar's death, and thereafter it has been given to William Walton, Benjamin Britten (who had previously refused a knighthood) and Michael Tippett. (Yehudi Menuhin, who as a child prodigy had played the Violin Concerto under Elgar's baton, also received the OM, but that was as a performer rather than as a composer.) In addition, Walton and Tippett were both knighted, Tippett was made a Companion of Honour, and Britten was additionally given not only the CH but eventually the peerage which had eluded Elgar, making him the most honoured British composer there has ever been. (Menuhin, like Britten, was also ennobled towards the end of his life.)[54] Here was a distinctly twentieth-century British trend: national honours for national composers, and Elgar was the first of the few.

III

For all his carefully cultivated self-image as a tortured, lonely, rejected, provincial outsider, it is clear that Elgar relished the recognition he received from the British sovereign and the British state, just as he prided himself on being (or, at least, on having become) a 'great gentleman'. Like his father, he was an instinctive monarchist as well as an instinctive Tory, and he was fully on the side of the established order and its institutions. When visiting London early in his career, Elgar used to put up at the Junior Conservative Club and when the Tories won the general election of July 1895, he was so delighted that according to Alice, 'he left his greatcoat and part of [his] suits on the train' (she does not specify which parts). He disliked Gladstone and his Irish Home Rule schemes, and he was well contented with the long years of Tory dominance from the mid-1880s to the mid-1900s. Not surprisingly, Elgar was dismayed by the Liberal landslide victory in the general election of 1906, which he lamented as 'installing the waiters in place of the gentlemen' and 'making the country no longer possible for respectable people'.[55] Six years later he was regretting that under Asquith's leadership '"Rule Britannia" has been made the most foolish of all national boasts', and in 1914 he signed the Ulster Covenant, which urged Ulstermen to go to any lengths to thwart the imposition of Home Rule by the Liberal Government. He was also much put out by trades union militancy, by the growth of 'socialistic' doctrines and by the advent and advance of the Labour Party: so much so that when Ramsay MacDonald was elected a member of the Athenaeum on becoming Prime Minister, he promptly resigned in protest. (Elgar detested MacDonald, but the Prime Minister behaved far more magnanimously, for it was during his second Labour government that he became a baronet.)

During Elgar's lifetime, the most visible and venerated British institution was the British Empire, and the years of his prime not only coincided with the efflorescence of civic pageantry and cere-monial and with the secular apotheosis of the monarchy, but also with the zenith of imperial expansion, consciousness and pride.[56] The year of Elgar's birth witnessed the Indian 'Mutiny', when the British just held on to the sub-continent and after which they eventually elaborated that extraordinary mode of government, by turns direct and indirect, bureaucratic and spectacular, that would be called the Raj. While Elgar was growing up, Disraeli proclaimed Queen Victoria Empress of India, annexed the island of Cyprus and purchased a major shareholding in the Suez Canal to safeguard the route to the east. The 'Scramble for Africa' began in earnest during the early 1880s, the continent was largely partitioned by the time of Victoria's Diamond Jubilee in 1897, and after the protracted battles of the Boer War, the British consolidated their last great dominion by creating the Union of South Africa in 1910. And in the immediate aftermath of the First World War, the British Empire reached its greatest territorial extent, as the Mandates held under the new League of Nations were in effect British colonies: among them Tanganyika, formerly German East Africa, which completed the all-red British route from the Cape to Cairo; and also Jordan and Iraq, which consolidated Britain's dominion in the Middle East.

Since Elgar was both a Conservative and a monarchist, and since the lower-middle classes were amongst the most fervent jingoists, it would seem both logical and chronological that he would also have been a staunch believer in, and a determined upholder of, the British Empire. 'In Elgar's Worcestershire', according to James Morris, 'the manifestations of imperial pride must have been inescapable': Clive of India and Warren Hastings both boasted Severn-side connections; the Worcester Regiments were regularly on overseas service; Alice Elgar had been born in India to a military-imperial family; and between his terms of office as Mayor of Worcester and Lord Steward of the Household, Lord Beauchamp had departed to Australia where he was Governor of New South Wales.[57] Moreover, some of Elgar's music undoubtedly reflected the contemporary preoccupation with empire. In 1897 he composed the *Imperial March* for Queen Victoria's Diamond Jubilee, and also *The Banner of St George*, whose epilogue celebrated Britain's 'empire of splendour'. The finale to *Caractacus*, which he produced the following year, urged Britons to be alert to the dangers their empire faced, and the XIIIth *Enigma Variation*, depicting Lady Mary Lygon, alludes to her impending journey to Australia where she would serve as her unmarried brother's hostess at Government House. In 1912 Elgar composed *The Crown of India*, a masque to celebrate George V's Delhi Durbar; during the First World War he produced *The Spirit of England* and *Fringes of the Fleet*; and there was the *Empire March* and *Pageant of Empire* for the Imperial Exhibition held at Wembley in 1924. In addition, Elgar was a regular participant in the annual observances of Empire Day during the 1920s, when he conducted the community singing in Hyde Park, which was led by Dame Clara Butt.[58]

Yet for a composer often derided during the inter-war years for being the quintessence of Edwardian imperial smugness, this is scarcely a substantial 'imperial' output.[59] The works Elgar wrote explicitly for imperial occasions are among the shortest and the slightest of his whole oeuvre. There are those who insist that the first *Pomp and Circumstance* march must be added, but the words associated with it were A. C. Benson's, and it is not clear that Elgar shared his hope that 'wider still and wider' should the bounds of the British Empire be set. Nor, *pace* James Morris, was Elgar's Worcestershire a county where imperial pride was particularly manifest: the region had produced no great proconsul since Warren Hastings, and the Severn was far less of an imperial waterway than the Clyde, the Tyne, the Mersey or the Thames.[60] Moreover, Elgar himself showed no interest in the British Empire or any inclination to visit it: he never went to Africa or India, Australia or New Zealand, and although he once crossed from the United States to Canada, he found Toronto an 'awful place', of 'vulgarity and general horror'.[61] Perhaps he had been put off the whole imperial venture when his former fiancée Helen Weaver emigrated to New Zealand to begin a new life after Elgar had broken off their engagement in 1885. It is also significant and suggestive that Elgar showed no inclination to network and to promote himself among imperialists in the way that he had done across the Severn Valley and at the royal court. And as he observed in a speech he delivered in Worcester in 1924, he had boundless sympathy for those who, for 'reasons which it is difficult to explain', had left the 'old city' to 'eke out a miserable existence in other parts of the Empire'.[62] These do not sound like the words of a man whose imagination had ever been captured by the allure of dominion over palm and pine, and it was thus wholly appropriate that all his royal and national honours were British, but none of them were Indian or imperial.

Elgar's essential lack of interest in the British Empire emerges more fully when he is compared with two of his close creative contemporaries, Rudyard Kipling and Edwin Lutyens: the laureate writer and the laureate architect to set alongside the laureate composer. Although they did not know each other well and moved in different social circles, they had important and revealing things in common. All three men were complex personalities, born in relatively humble circumstances, who were fiercely ambitious and married well—Kipling and Lutyens, indeed, better than Elgar, the former into the family of Burne-Jones and Stanley Baldwin, the latter to a daughter of Lord Lytton, who had been Disraeli's Viceroy of India.[63] All three were instinctive Tories, especially happy during the years 1885–1905, but they were seriously worried by the Liberal landslide of 1906, and Kipling joined Elgar in signing the Ulster Covenant in 1914.[64] All three possessed or established strong English territorial roots (Worcestershire for Elgar, Sussex for Kipling, the Home Counties for Lutyens); all three did national work during and after the First World War (Elgar with his song settings, Lutyens with his Cenotaph and cemeteries, and Kipling with his memorial inscriptions); and all three resented what they regarded as the levelling tendencies of the 1920s and 1930s, which meant they became increasingly out of touch and out of date. But there the resemblances end, for unlike Elgar, both Kipling and Lutyens travelled extensively in the British Empire, and they both made a lasting impact on it, Kipling through his Indian writings and Lutyens because of his work in New Delhi. By comparison, Elgar's interest in Britain's overseas dominions and possessions and his direct, personal impact on them, were both negligible. Unlike them, he was no bard of Empire, self-appointed or otherwise; indeed, he found much of Kipling's work repugnant, he set scarcely any of it to music, and he did not do so happily.[65]

To be sure, Elgar *did* possess a strong sense of the greater, broader, more challenging world beyond the shores of the British Isles; but for him, that world was not so much English-speaking and imperial as European and cosmopolitan, and it was, unsurprisingly, cultural rather than political. In 1883 he had first visited Leipzig, not to study music (which he could not then afford) but to hear concerts and attend the opera. Schumann and Wagner were much performed, and nearly a decade later, Elgar and his wife visited Bavaria and also Bayreuth. Thereafter, Elgar would visit Germany (and, increasingly, Italy) at every possible opportunity. He was at ease in continental concert halls, opera houses, restaurants and hotels; he was much influenced by the works of Schumann, Brahms, Dvořák and Wagner; there was a clear indebtedness by the Elgar of *Gerontius* to the Wagner of *Parsifal*; and when he came to compose his own symphonies and concertos, Elgar saw himself as belonging to, and seeking to embellish and carry forward, the great central-European orchestral tradition.[66] Although he spoke much of the importance of the Malvern Hills and the Severn Valley for his music, Elgar was not interested in English folk songs, in the way that Vaughan Williams, his successor as the nation's laureate composer, would be. Moreover, many of the friends he made, cultivated and networked with, once he had broken out of Worcester, were German or Jewish, or both: among them Jaeger, Richter, Speyer, Schuster and Rodewald. It was Richard Strauss who acclaimed Elgar as the foremost British composer of his generation and the Germans were initially more sympathetic to some of his works than were native audiences. Not surprisingly, Elgar was dismayed by the First World War, which set Britain and Germany against each other; although 'Land of Hope and Glory' was played more often than ever before, he failed to produce the additional, rousing, tub-thumping, imperialistic works that were popularly expected of him during the conflict; and his last months were darkened by his fear of what Hitler, who had recently gained power in Germany, might do to the Jews: 'my best and kindest friends'.[67]

Here, in essence, is a final, suggestive, and slightly subversive paradox of Elgar's life and work: the composer often accused of being a vulgar, chauvinistic jingo and a crude, unthinking imperialist turns out, on closer examination, to have been, among many other things, something of a mid-Victorian liberal internationalist.[68] This is hardly what might have been expected of someone who was the product of Tory, lower-middle-class, little-England Worcester; but Elgar was always a more complex and multi-layered figure than he at first sight appeared. In what has been called the inter-war age of extremes, he may have loathed 'blasted liberal rogues or liberals' (especially Ramsay MacDonald), but he was also clearly—and admirably—concerned about sinister recent developments in Nazi Germany.[69] He might have flourished in what has been called the age of empire, from the mid-1870s to the outbreak of the First World War, but even in his most *nobilmente* and ornamental mode, there was too much melancholy, too much 'stately sorrow', too much awareness of the transience of worldly power and earthy dominion in his music for him to be labelled an imperial propagandist.[70] And while he was brought up during the mid-Victorian years in what seemed to some, and seemed to Elgar, the close, closed, claustrophobic world of Worcester and the Severn Valley, and accepted unthinkingly many of its outlooks, prejudices, assumptions and presuppositions, he also seems to have sensed instinctively that there was a broader, bigger, better continental world of music and culture to which he was drawn, and to which he aspired to make his own distinctive contribution. In musical (and political) terms, Severn-side and nostalgia were undoubtedly a significant part of Elgar's life; but so in substantial measure were Europe and experimentation; and it was in his efforts to reconcile these aesthetic, geographical and ideological contradictions that he faced his greatest creative challenges.

From this perspective, the lights went out for Elgar in 1914, and they never came on again during his lifetime: for him, the major effect of the First World War was not that it set the bounds of the British Empire 'wider still and wider' than ever before, but that it had brought to an end the cosmopolitan world of European culture of which the fulcrum had been amicable and fruitful Anglo-German relations. This catastrophe, at least as much as the death of his wife, helps explain why Elgar suddenly stopped composing after the Cello Concerto; and nor was he alone among late-Romantic composers in outliving his own inspiration, for among his contemporaries, Dukas, Sibelius, Ives and Rachmaninov were similarly stricken.[71] In 1921, Elgar sold Severn House in London and he now began winding down his life. Two years later he returned and effectively retired to Worcestershire, where he now became a fixture at the city's civic functions and at the Three Choirs Festival, clad either in court dress with his sashes and stars, or in a three piece suit with a bowler hat: a gentleman first, a military-looking man second, and a composer a long way third. (Is it just coincidence that Colonel Blimp was invented by David Low in 1934, the very year of Elgar's death?)[72] The younger generation, including Siegfried Sassoon, Constant Lambert and Osbert Sitwell, derided Elgar as an Edwardian anachronism whose music was irremediably pompous, smug and vulgar, and his symphonies and his concertos were performed, if they were performed at all, in half-empty concert halls. As the last verse of *The Music-Makers* had predicted, with inadvertent clairvoyance, Elgar was now 'a dreamer who slumbers and a singer who sings no more'; he had, he observed in 1927, the year in which he turned seventy, and in what still seems an astonishing remark, 'no pleasant memories of music'.[73]

Yet as so often with Elgar, the picture was more complex than his own selective presentation of it would suggest. In a nation governed by the 'respectable tendency' of the inter-war years and embodied in the august personages of Archbishop Cosmo Gordon Lang and King George V himself, there was still a large and appreciative audience for Elgar's work: the concert halls may not have been full, but his music was championed by such young conductors as Malcolm Sargent and Adrian Boult and was more widely performed than that of the new progressive generation of composers; and thanks to the gramophone and the wireless, his songs and symphonies and concertos were a more pervasive element in British life and culture than they had ever been before.[74] As a result, his income remained buoyant, and it was further augmented by the proceeds of the sale of Severn House and by the legacies from his wife and Frank Schuster; another reason why Elgar stopped composing during the 1920s may have been that he no longer needed the money. Nor had he become the forgotten figure he claimed he now was: he kept a flat in London and was often seen in the capital, while the honours continued to cascade in. And Elgar's Severn-side world, of county towns, manor houses and rural rectories, of Tory emollience and pre-1914 nostalgia, was more than ever intruded into the nation's public consciousness and cultural life at this time: via the best-selling novels of Francis Brett Young, which evoked precisely 'this little world'; via the eirenic rhetoric of another Worcestershire man, Stanley Baldwin, who was the dominant politician of the era; and via the works of P. G. Wodehouse, who situated Blandings Castle in Shropshire and provided it with an owner, Lord Emsworth, whom Elgar himself in some ways closely resembled.[75] From this perspective, Elgar was not a marginal man in the final phase of his life; on the contrary, in some ways his culture had become the whole nation's culture, and the prevailing mood was domestic, wounded and introverted rather than bombastic, confident and imperial. Indeed, by the 1920s, his music was more associated with Armistice Day than with Empire Day.[76]

IV

No wonder Elgar's death in 1934 was greeted with the proposal by the Dean of Westminster of burial in the Abbey: the ultimate accolade of establishment acceptance and veneration. The offer was refused, and Elgar was laid to rest next to his wife in the graveyard of St Wulstan's Church in Little Malvern. But a memorial service was held in Worcester Cathedral, where a stained-glass window commemorating his life was subsequently dedicated; and in 1972 Elgar was eventually honoured in Westminster Abbey, where a memorial tablet was unveiled in the north choir aisle by the then prime minister, Edward Heath.[77] These were scarcely the obsequies of an obscure Worcestershire man, nor those of a tortured, rejected, disappointed outsider: on the contrary, they were a measure of Elgar's remarkable success in conquering the world. In so skilfully intertwining his ambition and his creativity, his networking and his composing, his letter-writing and his music-making, Elgar had orchestrated his life to perfection, overcoming obstacles, setbacks and disappointments that would have discouraged a lesser man: for Elgar was as determined as he was talented, and this was a formidable combination of attributes. And once he had achieved the success he sought and the recognition he craved, there were no more worlds left for him to conquer (least of all the Empire). From this perspective, it then becomes plain why and how Elgar's creativity tailed off some years before the First World War or the death of his wife, or the recording and the broadcasting of his work. As he himself put it, on receiving the Order of Merit, just after the Second Symphony had premiered in 1911, what else was there left for him to achieve?[78] What, indeed?

Yet the more it recedes into the distance, and the more we are able to understand just how he did it, the more extraordinary the trajectory of Elgar's career now seems. He certainly suffered fewer youthful disadvantages than he subsequently claimed, but none of the major English composers who have come after him had to travel so large a distance from obscurity to recognition as he did, or labour so hard to do so, or created the laureate niche they would eventually occupy. Consider, in this regard, those who, following the precedent that Elgar himself established, were subsequently awarded the Order of Merit. Ralph Vaughan Williams was exceptionally well-connected, with relatives among the Wedgwood and the Darwin families, and he was educated at Trinity College, Cambridge and the Royal College of Music. William Walton might have come from grimy, depressed and provincial Oldham, but he won a scholarship to the choir school of Christ Church, Oxford, and from an early age he enjoyed the lavish patronage of the Sitwells and other aristocratic families.[79] Benjamin Britten received a privileged education at Gresham's School, Holt, and like Vaughan Williams went on to study at the Royal College of Music. And Michael Tippett's father was a lawyer and businessman, and he himself attended public school, namely Fettes College, before going on to study at the Royal College.[80] In short, none of Elgar's successors as laureate composers came from such lowly beginnings, or had to work so tirelessly to overcome them, as he did. Moreover, none of them sought honours as ardently as he did, and none of them held political views which were so conventionally Conservative. This cannot be coincidence.

Of course, Elgar's best compositions have long since taken their rightful place among the last great flowerings of late-nineteenth- and early-twentieth-century European romanticism, and they are far more continental in their inspiration, and cosmopolitan in their allusions, than portraits of him as the 'spirit of England' are minded to suggest or willing to appreciate. Moreover, his laureate compositions are now rightly seen not only as the product of a particular period of municipal grandeur, royal veneration and imperial pride, but also as being, in their lyrical melancholy, far less bombastic and jingoistic than his critics have alleged. This was the time-bound, place-specific environment in which Elgar resolved to make his way, and he succeeded brilliantly: partly because he was an able businessman who cared about money and knew how to make it; partly because he was indeed a great artist, whose soul and spirit were touched by genius; and partly because he wanted to be both a composer and a gentleman, and regarded the former as the essential route to the latter. Since Elgar's death, the world in which he lived and worked (and networked) has largely vanished, even as the music whereby he transcended it has lived on and on and on. Yet if we are to grasp the full measure of Elgar's achievement, the history of his music is inseparable from the history of his life, and neither can be understood without reference to the history of his times. In more senses than one, Elgar was, indeed, a historical personality, and the more his world recedes into the distance, the more of a historical personality he becomes with each passing year.

Notes

1 This essay has been gestating for a long time, and I am deeply grateful to many friends and colleagues who have helped it (and me) along the way: Stephen Banfield, Derek Beales, Jim Berrow, Richard Carrick, Ernest Dale, the late Cyril Erlich, Ludmilla Jordanova, Nicholas Kenyon, Nomi Levy-Carrick, Helen McCarthy, Patrick McCarthy, Peter Mandler, Roy Massey, Rosalind Morrison, Carl Newton, Robin Whittaker and David Wright. Earlier versions have been given to the History of Music Seminar at the Institute of Historical Research, as the Local History Week Lecture in Worcester, as a Humanities Lecture at the University of Greenwich, and as the keynote address to a conference on history and music held at the Centre for Research in the Arts, Humanities and Social Sciences at the University of Cambridge. Most of the details of Elgar's life and times are very well known, so I have only provided references for specific quotations from his correspondence, and also to broader historical works where necessary.

2 In thinking about these matters, I have been much helped by M. Wilson, 'Rebels and Martyrs', and by R. Christiansen, 'Imaging the Artist: Painters and Sculptors in Nineteenth-Century Literature', both in A. Sturgis *et al.*, *Rebels and Martyrs: The Image of the Artist in the Nineteenth Century* (London, 2006), pp. 6–29, 30–41.

3 K. Clark, *Civilisation: A Personal View* (London, 1971), p. 347. This is also a
favourite self-image of public (and not-so-public) intellectuals, for which see S.
Collini, *Absent Minds: Intellectuals in Britain* (Oxford, 2006), pp. 413–34.

4 J. N. Moore, *Edward Elgar: A Creative Life* (London, 1984), pp. 259, 334, 351,
458, 563, 638, 814.

5 M. De-la-Noy, *Elgar: The Man* (London, 1983), p. 27.

6 B.Maine, *Elgar: His Life and Works* (2 vols, London: Bell, 1933); P. M. Young,
Elgar, OM: A Study of a Musician (London, 1935); D. McVeagh, *Edward Elgar:
His Life and Music* (London, 1955); J. N. Moore, *Spirit of England: Edward
Elgar and his World* (London, 1984), esp. pp. 15, 60; *idem, Elgar*, pp. vii-viii;
De-la-Noy, *Elgar: The Man*, pp. 11–14, 235; M. Kennedy, *Portrait of Elgar* (3rd
edn, London, 1987), pp. 124, 186.

7 P. M. Young (ed.), *Letters of Elgar and Other Writings* (London, 1956),
p. 305.

8 Moore, *Spirit of England*, p. 146.

9 J. MacLeod, *The Sisters d'Aranyi* (London, 1969), p. 118; M. Hughes, 'The Duc
d'Elgar: Making of a Composer a Gentleman', in C. Norris (ed.), *Music and the
Politics of Culture* (London, 1989), pp. 41–68; D. Hague-Holmes, 'Elgar and the
Class Society', *The Elgar Society Journal*, September 1993, 114–18; January
1994, 152–7.

10 Kennedy, *Portrait of Elgar*, p. 305.

11 K. T. Hoppen, *The Mid-Victorian Generation, 1846–1886* (Oxford, 1998),
pp. 372–426.

12 C. Newton, '"Now He Belongs to the Big World": The Historical Elgar', in K. D.
Michell (ed.), *Cockaigne: Essays on Elgar 'In London Town'* (Rickmansworth,
2004), pp. 69–73.

13 The pioneering work in this regard is Newton, 'The Historical Elgar', esp.
pp. 58–62, to which I am much indebted.

14 J. N. Moore (ed.), *Edward Elgar: Letters of a Lifetime* (Oxford, 1990),
p. 272.

15 Kennedy, *Portrait of Elgar*, pp. 15–16.

16 W. L. Burn, *The Age of Equipoise: A Study of the Mid-Victorian Generation*
(London, 1968), p. 7; A. Briggs, *Victorian Cities* (Harmondsworth, 1968),
pp. 361–80; A. Armstrong, *Stability and Change in an English County Town: A
Social Study of York, 1801–1851* (Cambridge, 1974), p. 10.

17 There is, regrettably, no study of nineteenth-century Worcester to compare with,
for instance: R. Newton, *Victorian Exeter, 1830–1910* (Leicester, 1968); F. Hill,
Victorian Lincoln (Cambridge, 1974).

18 J. N. Moore (ed.), *Elgar and His Publishers: Letters of a Creative Life* (2 Vols,
Oxford: Clarendon, 1987), vol. I, p. 240; R. Burley and F. C. Carruthers,
Edward Elgar: The Record of a Friendship (London: Barrie and Jenkins, 1972),
p. 148.

19 T. Vigne and A. Howkins, 'The Small Shopkeeper in Industrial and Market
Towns', in G. J. Crossick (ed.), *The Lower Middle Class in Britain, 1870–1914*
(London, 1977), pp. 184–209; Newton, 'The Historical Elgar', p. 64.

20 A. J. Mayer, 'The Lower Middle Class as Historical Problem', *Journal of Modern
History*, XLVII (1975), 409–36; G. J. Crossick, 'The Emergence of the Lower
Middle Class in Britain: A Discussion', in Crossick, *Lower Middle Class*, pp. 12,
15–17.

21 Moore, *Letters of a Lifetime*, p. 292; idem, *A Creative Life*, pp. 38–40.
22 Young, *Letters of Edward Elgar*, p. 304; H. A. Leicester, *Notes on Catholic Worcester* (Worcester, 1928); idem, *Forgotten Worcester* (Worcester, 1930); idem, *Worcester Remembered* (Worcester, 1935); W. G. Benham, *Ancient Legends Concerned with the Arms of Colchester* (Colchester, 1901); idem, *Colchester Oyster Feast* (Colchester, 1901); idem, *Colchester Castle* (Colchester, 1935); idem, *The Roman City of Camulodunum* (Colchester, 1937).
23 D. Cannadine, 'The Transformation of Civic Ritual in Modern Britain: The Colchester Oyster Feast', *Past & Present*, no. 94 (1982), 113–22; idem, 'The Brief Flowering of a Civic Religion', *The Listener*, 26 July 1984, 14–15; D. Cannadine and E. Hammerton, 'Conflict and Consensus on a Ceremonial Occasion: The Diamond Jubilee in Cambridge', *Historical Journal*, XXIV (1981), 111–46; T. B. Smith, 'In Defence of Privilege: The City of London and the Challenge of Municipal Reform, 1875–1890', *Journal of Social History*, XXVII (1993–94), 59–83.
24 Moore, *A Creative Life*, p. 771.
25 *VCH Worcestershire*, vol. II (London, 1906), pp. 197–211, 234–7.
26 N. Pevsner, *The Buildings of England: Worcestershire* (Harmondsworth, 1968), p. 323; Kennedy, *Portrait of Elgar*, p. 164.
27 M. Girouard, *The Return to Camelot: Chivalry and the English Gentleman* (London, 1981), pp. 56–66.
28 Quoted in C. Schorske, *Fin-de-Siècle Vienna: Politics and Culture* (New York, 1980), p. 359; Mayer, 'The Lower Middle Class', p. 436.
29 H. J. Hanham, *Elections and Party Management: Politics in the Time of Disraeli and Gladstone* (Hassocks, 1978), pp. 263, 267, 281–3; H. Pelling, *Social Geography of British Elections, 1885–1910* (London, 1967), pp. 188, 192–3, 429; Moore, *Letters of a Lifetime*, p. 174.
30 A. D. Dyer, *The City of Worcester in the Sixteenth Century* (Leicester, 1973), p. 255; Kennedy, *Portrait of Elgar*, p.165.
31 T. C. Turberville, *Worcestershire in the Nineteenth Century* (London, 1852), pp. 312–27; *VCH Worcestershire*, vol. I (London, 1901), p. xiii; *VCH Worcestershire*, vol. II, pp. 198, 228–34; Pevsner, *Worcestershire*, pp. 24, 28, 38–40.
32 F. M. L. Thompson, *English Landed Society in the Nineteenth Century* (London, 1963), pp. 29–33, 113–8; Pelling, *Social Geography*, pp. 116–7, 155, 190–1, 198–201.
33 C. L. Graves, *Hubert Parry: His Life and Works* (2 vols, London, 1926), vol. I, pp. 1–14; J. Bateman, *The Great Landowners of Great Britain and Ireland* (4th edn, London, 1883, ed. D. Spring, Leicester), p. 352; S. Banfield, 'The Artist and Society', in N. Temperley (ed.), *Music in Britain: The Romantic Age, 1800–1914* (London, 1981), p. 27.
34 A. Boden, *Three Choirs: A History of the Festival—Gloucester, Hereford, Worcester* (1992), pp. 61, 113; Moore, *Spirit of England*, pp. 25–6; Kennedy, *Portrait of Elgar*, pp. 45, 61, 72.
35 P. M. Young, *Alice Elgar: Enigma of a Victorian Lady* (London: Dobson, 1978), pp. 15–47.
36 M. Wilson, 'Rebels and Martyrs', p. 13.
37 Moore, *Spirit of England*, pp. 30–6; idem, *Elgar: A Creative Life*, pp. 247–6; Kennedy, *Portrait of Elgar*, pp. 90–9.
38 J. Ridley, *Lord Palmerston* (London, 1970), pp. 523–4.
39 Quoted in Burn, *Age of Equipoise*, p. 105.

40 Burley and Carruthers, *Elgar: Record of a Friendship*, p. 26.
41 Newton, 'The Historical Elgar', p. 67; F. Musgrove, 'The Rise of a Northern Musical Elite', *Northern History*, XXXV (1999), 50–76.
42 W. O. Chadwick, *The Victorian Church*, pt. II (London, 1970), pp. 402–7; G. I. T. Machin, *Politics and the Churches in Great Britain, 1869 to 1921* (Oxford, 1987), pp. 114–7, 161–4, 202–4, 217–8, 276.
43 *VCH Worcestershire*, Vol. II, p. 227.
44 Mayer, 'The Lower Middle Class', p. 424; Pevsner, *Worcestershire*, p. 323.
45 D. Cannadine, 'The Context, Performance and Meaning of Ritual: The British Monarchy and the "Invention of Tradition", *c.* 1820–1977', in E. Hobsbawm and T. Ranger (eds), *The Invention of Tradition* (Cambridge, 1983), pp. 101–64.
46 Moore, *Letters of a Lifetime*, p. 134.
47 Kennedy, *Portrait of Elgar*, p. 305; J. N. Moore, *Elgar: The Windflower Letters* (Oxford, 1989), p. 290.
48 D. Cannadine, *The Decline and Fall of the British Aristocracy* (London, 1990), pp. 299–325; idem, *Ornamentalism: How the British Saw Their Empire* (London, 2002), pp. 85–100.
49 De-la-Noy, *Elgar: The Man*, p. 161.
50 Burley and Carruthers, *Elgar: Record of a Friendship*, pp. 174, 202.
51 Moore, *Windflower Letters*, p. 117.
52 Moore, *Windflower Letters*, p. 284.
53 U. Vaughan Williams, *R.V.W: A Biography of Ralph Vaughan Williams* (Oxford, 1988), p. 322.
54 Vaughan Williams, *R.V.W.*, pp. 206–7; M. Kennedy, *Portrait of Walton* (Oxford, 1990), pp. 150, 235; H. Carpenter, *Benjamin Britten: A Biography* (London, 1992), pp. 318, 448, 579; H. Burton, *Menuhin: A Life* (London, 2000), pp. 130–5, 358, 424, 462–3, 473–5.
55 De-la-Noy, *Elgar: The Man*, pp. 47, 62, 139–40; Moore, *Letters of a Lifetime*, p. 249.
56 Cannadine, *Ornamentalism*, pp. 101–20.
57 R. Price, 'Society, Status and Jingoism: The Social Roots of Lower-Middle-Class Patriotism, 1870–1900', in Crossick, *Lower Middle Class*, pp. 89–112; J. Morris, *Pax Britannica: The Climax of an Empire* (London, 1968), pp. 341–2.
58 J. M. MacKenzie, 'In Touch with the Infinite: the BBC and the Empire, 1923–53', in J. M. MacKenzie (ed.), *Imperialism and Popular Culture* (Manchester, 1986), p. 169.
59 I am here following the arguments outlined in: B. Porter, 'Edward Elgar and Empire', *Journal of Imperial and Commonwealth History*, XXIX (2001), 1–34; idem, 'Pompous and Circumstantial: Elgar and Empire', in W. R. Louis (ed.), *Still More Adventures with Britannia: Personalities, Politics and Culture in Britain* (London, 2003), pp. 19–32. For the alternative view, that Elgar's work was drenched in imperial hubris and ideology, see J. Richard, *Imperialism and Music: Britain, 1876–1953* (Manchester, 2001), pp. 44–87.
60 *VCH Worcestershire*, vol. II, p. 227.
61 Moore, *Elgar: A Creative Life*, p. 612.
62 Moore, *Elgar: A Creative Life*, p. 770.
63 J. Ridley, *The Architect and His Wife: A Life of Edwin Lutyens* (London, 2002), pp. 81–116.

64 D. Gilmour, *The Long Recessional: The Imperial Life of Rudyard Kipling* (London, 2002), p. 246.

65 B. Porter, *The Absent-Minded Imperialists: Empire, Society and Culture in Britain* (Oxford, 2004), p. 251. But *cf.* Richard, *Imperialism and Music*, pp. 51–5.

66 D. Mitchell, 'The Composer Among the Monuments', *TLS*, 14 September 1984, pp. 1011–2.

67 Neill, 'Elgar's Creative Challenge', in L. Foreman (ed.), *Oh, My Horses! Elgar and the Great War* (Rickmansworth, 2001), pp. 216–39; Moore, *Letters of a Lifetime*, pp. 466–7.

68 D. E. D. Beales, *From Castlereagh to Gladstone, 1815–1885* (London, 1969), p. 279.

69 Moore, *Elgar and His Publishers*, Vol. II, p. 860.

70 E. Newman, 'Stately Sorrow: On the Music of Sir Edward Elgar', in F. Aprahamian (ed.), *Essays on Music: an Anthology from 'The Listener'* (London, 1967), p. 101.

71 D. Cannadine, *The Pleasures of the Past* (London, 1989), p. 130.

72 Bolden, *Three Choirs*, pp. 162–81; P. Mandler, *The English National Character: The History of an Idea from Edmund Burke to Tony Blair* (London, 2006), p. 182.

73 Kennedy, *Portrait of Elgar*, pp. 306–7.

74 A. Roberts, *The 'Holy Fox': A Biography of Lord Halifax* (London, 1991), p. 305; R. Aldous, *Tunes of Glory: The Life of Malcolm Sargent* (London, 2002), p. 124; J. Crump, 'The Identity of English Music: The Reception of Elgar, 1898–1935', in R. Colls and P. Dodd (eds), *Englishness: Politics and Culture* (London, 1986), pp. 178–85; R. Taylor, 'Music in the Air: Elgar and the BBC', in R. Monck (ed.), *Edward Elgar: Music and Literature* (Aldershot, 1993), pp. 327–5; J. Gardiner, 'The Reception of Sir Edward Elgar, 1918–*c*.1934: A Reassessment', *Twentieth-Century British History*, IX (1998), 370–95.

75 Newton, 'The Historical Elgar', p. 71; D. Cannadine, *In Churchill's Shadow: Confronting the Past in Modern Britain* (London, 2003), pp. 159–85.

76 Gardiner, 'Reception of Sir Edward Elgar', p. 385.

77 De-la-Noy, *Elgar: The Man*, pp. 233–5.

78 McVeagh, *Elgar: His Life and Music*, p. 55.

79 N. Annan, 'The Intellectual Aristocracy', in J. H. Plumb (ed.), *Studies in Social History: A Tribute to G.M.Trevelyan* (London, 1955), p. 265; Kennedy, *Portrait of Walton*, pp. 6–10, 14–21.

80 M. Bowen, *Michael Tippett* (London, 1982), pp. 15–7; I. Kemp, *Tippett: The Composer and His Music* (London, 1984), pp. 1–13; M. Tippett, *Those Twentieth-Century Blues: An Autobiography* (London, 1991), pp. 1–11.

2

Elgar's Biography, Elgar's Repute: Themes and Variations

JULIAN RUSHTON

Elgar's earliest biographers were properly constrained by the tact appropriate for a living subject, or his remaining contemporaries. Biographies written in his first years of fame possess less scholarly than documentary interest, and were designed partly as propaganda for the cause of (in Richard Strauss's words of 1902), 'the first English progressivist'. The memories of friends tended to confirm Elgar's status as a national icon, against the prevailing trend that unfairly relegated him to a discredited Edwardian past. Among the friendly reminiscences still worth consulting are those of W. H. ('Billy') Reed, a professional associate and friend, who wrote a 'Master Musicians' study as well as personal reminiscences.[1] An earlier phase in Elgar's career is intimately chronicled in a widely-read book by Dora Penny (Mrs Richard Powell: 'Dorabella' of the 'Enigma' variations).[2] More controversial, and revealing about still earlier years, are the memories of Rosa Burley, which could only appear after inhibitions of the *de mortuis nil nisi bonum* type had ceased to apply in our culture.[3] Burley offered an Elgar with warts, alternately depressed and exuberant, and refreshingly remote from the carefully constructed stiff-upper-lipped persona of an English gentleman with a remarkable moustache and the temper of an imperialist. She provided a wholesome reminder of Elgar's origins and early struggles for opportunity and recognition. If she implied (with her quip that, not being a variation, she was the theme) an intimacy that might not have been entirely proper, it may have been belated revenge for being dropped socially, presumably at Lady Elgar's instigation. A more playful Elgar emerges from Wulstan Atkins's publication of a book based around letters between Elgar and his father Ivor, another fellow-professional.[4] It needed the resources of scholarly biography to reconcile such diverse portraits and depict more fully the complexity of the over-sized personality glimpsed through them.

Elgar's eminence was sufficient for the first substantial literary and scholarly biography to appear in his lifetime, in two volumes, by Basil Maine. Then there was an interlude, coinciding with the nadir of the composer's reputation. It was the strengths of Elgar's music that prevented him from fading into the historical tapestry woven of reputations over-inflated in their lifetimes, like those of Spohr or Parry. The major contribution to his subsequent revival was through performance, but musical criticism and biography played their part. Particular credit must go to the first modern biographical and (still more importantly) musical studies, by Diana McVeagh and Percy M. Young, both published in 1955, and each consisting of a relatively concise biography followed by studies of the works, organized by genre.[5] Neither could be affected by Burley's reminiscences, although Young's chronicle of Elgar's life mentions her in passing. This substantial book includes a delightful musical supplement with 'The Moods of [Bulldog] Dan', but while thoroughly researched, it has little in the way of interpretation. Perhaps it was too soon, with too many of the composer's acquaintance still living, for the author to get behind the public persona. Nevertheless these books signalled a post-war re-evaluation of Elgar, helped along by the existence of long-playing records (some of Elgar's own recordings were quickly transferred to LP).

McVeagh's book is weighted more heavily towards the music, and for that reason may be considered one of the main foundation-stones of modern Elgar studies. McVeagh is no hagiographer; she is not afraid to discriminate between what she perceives as strong and weak, opening one chapter crisply with 'Elgar wrote no excellent and not a few bad solo songs' (p. 137). She discusses his weak choice of poetry and peculiarities of word-setting in terms that reflect the period of the Purcell revival and the Purcell-influenced songs of Britten and Tippett. Sharp observations on the unevenness of the Piano Quintet (p. 176) might arouse more emphatic dissent; not everyone agrees (although I do) in preferring the String Quartet. An admirable feature is her incisive discussion of orchestration, never an easy subject to write about. But conclusions about McVeagh's work are premature; a new book on Elgar's music is scheduled for 2007, and she may well have changed her views.[6] Indeed, with fifty more years of affectionate engagement with the music, it would be odd if she did not. Meanwhile her early examination of the composer is still readable with profit, as is her Elgar article in *The New Grove Dictionary*.

McVeagh's 1955 book is comparable in scope to her publisher's (Dent's) *Master Musicians*, but the official replacement for Reed's pre-war volume was by Ian Parrott, a short book somewhat distended by a whole chapter outlining an improbable 'solution' to the 'enigma'.[7] This in turn was replaced by a much longer volume by Robert Anderson.[8] Since that time the *Master Musicians* volumes have been slimmed down; fortunately there can be no immediate need to replace Anderson's comprehensive and sober study. The series has also passed into the hands of Oxford University Press, which had already published two epoch-marking studies of the composer.

The first was Michael Kennedy's, significantly called a 'portrait' of Elgar.[9] Perhaps taking a lead from McVeagh's 'highly-strung' composer (p. 88), Kennedy's psychological approach is symbolized by the cover to the third edition: not a portrait of a public Elgar, dynamic, spiritual (composing *Gerontius*), or splendidly moustached and ostensibly prosperous, but the private individual shown in a delicate watercolour of 1915: a leaner-looking Elgar, a little wrinkled, perhaps a little depressed (why not, at this juncture in the war?). Rather than 'life then works', Kennedy adopts a structure in which comments on the music are built into the chronological narrative, without the kind of analysis that can only be supported by extensive music examples; only a few melodies are notated, but the work is analytical mainly in human terms.

Kennedy has attracted criticism for letting his subjects, including Elgar and Richard Strauss, off the hooks devised by political retrospection: in Strauss's case, the Nazi hook, in Elgar's, imperialism. A more recent biographer has pointed out that Elgar was not born in a class much concerned with Empire; rather, he married into imperialism (admittedly, as husbands often do, he went along with it to some extent).[10] The argument about Elgar's imperial commitment, fuelled by *The Banner of St George* and the closing pages of *Caractacus*, may never die, although his remark apropos the latter—'England for the English is all I say'—is if anything the reverse of imperialistic.[11] His most overtly imperialist work, *The Crown of India*, may be representative of his views or merely an opportunity, thanks to the music hall, to make a better income than he could with better works:

> When I write a big serious work e.g. Gerontius we have had to starve & go without fires . . . this small effort allows me to buy scientific works I have yearned for & I spend my time between the Coliseum & the old bookshops.[12]

Elgar was much travelled, but not to any part of the Empire; his indifference to non-European music showed when he recycled parts of a piano piece, *In Smyrna* (then an Ottoman city of largely Greek population), to evoke the mysterious East in *The Crown of India*. Elgar is censured for complicity with movements that, in his own time, were not culturally marginalized and were seldom seen as deplorable as, apparently, they are today.[13] I say 'apparently' because, Empire aside, Elgar's Toryism—a tendency seldom represented in the community of modern writers on the politics of art—is hard to separate from the UK's main governing party throughout the twentieth century, to 1997 (some would say beyond).

Commentary on Elgar, and others, from perspectives opened up by, for instance, Edward Said, can produce valuable insights so long as it avoids the 'holier than thou' postures (whatever their ideological basis) that can disfigure 'new' musicology. The subject is unlikely to rest: a trenchant refutation of the division, promoted by Kennedy, between an 'imperial' and an 'aesthetic' Elgar emerged at the 2006 congress of the American Musicological Society.[14] Kennedy does not, of course, deny the national sentiment evident in many works, such as *The Spirit of England*. But his main achievement was to shine a sympathetic but unsparing torch onto Elgar's crotchety personality. Mood swings are abundantly documented in his letters, and Kennedy carefully evaluates their contexts and causes; and he examines the mood swings within the music itself. An Elgar emerges whose major works are complex, like the man himself; seldom guilty of complacency; and frequently ambiguous in what may crudely be considered their narrative trajectory. Kennedy's version of Elgar, even if it may be modified, is likely in large part to endure, for it is a rounded view of a late romantic and early modernist composer at the heart of European musical developments, and a man whose inner life was often at odds with a carefully constructed public image. Its importance is signalled by three editions of *Portrait of Elgar* prior to a more recent and shorter life.[15]

Kennedy's was not a heavily documented biography comparable to Thayer's *Beethoven* or Ernest Newman's *Wagner*. Work comparable to these scholarly landmarks was undertaken by Jerrold Northrop Moore. Although his life of Elgar does not expand to rival Newman's four volumes, he has supplemented his work by editing four volumes of Elgar's letters.[16] It is likely to remain standard, because of its almost day by day reconstruction of what was going on in Elgar's life. Moore gets close enough to his subject to refer to him throughout as 'Edward'—a familiarity unusual in his lifetime (the cover portrait, from 1904, the moustache reaching towards the ears and untinged by grey, the eyes directed both at and beyond the viewer to something more numinous, is hardly an invitation to intimacy). Like Kennedy, Moore treats the music chronologically, within the narrative, and with far more music type. Musicians have detected some naivety, and perhaps optimism, in pointing up connections between works (and those to a very early notation made by the boy Elgar) that may be imperceptible to scepticism, but the depth of his musical engagement is not in doubt.

In tracing the origins of Elgar's character and musical inspiration, Moore places considerable emphasis on his physical environment, the 'Three Choirs' counties in which he walked and cycled; a more recent, less formal, study increases this emphasis, producing an image of Elgar as 'pastoral visionary' supported by numerous comments, not to mention habits, of the composer himself.[17] None can doubt Elgar's love of the vale of the Severn, the Malvern hills, the trees that make up an English landscape; he told A. J. Jaeger that he underlined his tragic hero Caractacus's sense of loss by having him choke on 'woodlands'.[18] But Elgar's ambience included townscapes: when young he lived mainly in Worcester, not at his birthplace, Broadheath; subsequently he lived in Malvern, Hereford and London, occasionally retreating to the country for concentrated work on composition. He composed *Cockaigne* as a cordial tribute to the capital, and planned, but eventually abandoned, a companion, or anti-Cockaigne, overture, *City of Dreadful Night*. When young, he visited London assiduously, educating himself by attending concerts. One aspect of Elgar's divine discontent was that he needed, yet did not really like, London. He was also much travelled, in Europe and elsewhere, for recreation, to recharge his musical batteries and to hear and direct performances, mainly in towns. The urban Elgar is no less essential than the pastoral. He mixed sociability with social ineptitude, sometimes downright rudeness; and he is also partly defined by his circle—or his intersecting circles—of acquaintance. This important point has led to a spread of publications from the picturesque ('Elgar in Giggleswick') to interpretation, sometimes caustic, of his social climbing. This was not only Lady Elgar's; after her death he lobbied successfully to become Master of the King's Musick, and unsuccessfully for a peerage. Such aspirations are easily mocked, and the last was peculiarly unlikely to happen. But Elgar's motivation may have been to some extent altruistic, especially as he had no male heir to receive the title after his death. The only person so far offered a (life) peerage for the excellence of his compositions, Benjamin Britten, seems to have accepted for the sake of the profession; Elgar was certainly no less concerned to raise the status of music and musicians.[19]

Moore contributes much to the received idea of Elgar as the quintessence of Englishness; perhaps too much. For Elgar the musician was quintessentially European; the only reason his music sounds English is that it sounds like Elgar, whom we know to be English, and he naturally wrote an *Imperial March*, rather than (as with Wagner) a *Kaisermarsch*. Elgar's music is markedly different from composers whose work is rooted in national *musical* traditions, like Grieg, Vaughan Williams or Bartók. His lack of insularity, as well as his astonishing orchestral technique and the drive and flow of his invention, was responsible for his rapid acceptance abroad, at least in Germany, where he might have stood shoulder to shoulder with Mahler and Strauss as an example of early European modernism. Some specificity in landscape—as with Strauss's *Alpine Symphony*—is only to be expected, but like Strauss, and his Scandinavian contemporaries Sibelius and Nielsen, he was also inspired by Italy. His music, too, was fuelled by a thoroughly healthy eclecticism. His visits to Bayreuth are rightly remembered, but he also liked Italian opera, no doubt hearing something kindred in Puccini's dramatically sensitive and idiomatic orchestration (as distinct from Parry's, 'an *organ part arranged*').[20] Among older composers he admired not only Schumann and Brahms but also what he knew of Berlioz, and he played under Dvořák and delighted in his music. From these diverse musical influences came the ability to realize the inspiration of a glint of sunshine on the confluence of the Severn and the Teme. But Moore is not wrong to conclude that in common with other artists (not only Proust), Elgar's music sought 'the illumination of time remembered'.[21] And Moore's own work, for the richness of its solidly documented narrative, will continue to be well-thumbed by Elgar enthusiasts—and scholars.

An alternative model for building a comprehensive picture of a life and works is the essay collection, a more or less thematic gathering of specialized studies of the music and of Elgar's cultural ambience (excluding neither the pastoral nor his alleged imperialism). This format is perhaps favoured by a younger generation but is by no means new. The enterprise of Raymond Monk produced two volumes that include several original studies. The late Peter Dennison, on Elgar's apprenticeship, slightly over-favours the influence of Wagner; Diana McVeagh raised understanding of *Falstaff* to the point where, once again, it is considered one of Elgar's greatest works; K. E. L. Simmons drew attention to a neglected area in a study of *The Starlight Express*; Robert Anderson wrote about Elgar's plans for completing the *Apostles* trilogy.[22] In the second collection Christopher Kent enlarges knowledge of *Falstaff* through sketches; but this book, subtitled 'Music and Literature', is dominated by Brian Trowell's magnificent 140-page study of exactly that: 'Elgar's use of literature'.[23] After Dent, Oxford, and the Scolar Press, Cambridge University Press could hardly be left out; Elgar is included in its growing parallel series of multi-authored composer companions and composer studies; a significant pointer to Elgar's future reputation may be the inclusion of a number of American authors.[24] One eagerly-awaited volume, part of another series of essays on composers, will be *Elgar and his World*.[25]

Collecting in a book material scattered in various kinds of journal is another kind of publication that contributes to the solid foundation of reception history, both from the composer's lifetime and subsequently; one such is Christopher Redwood's collection of over forty reviews and articles, the earliest from the 1890s, many of them only a few pages long but including the first published interview with Elgar.[26] Recently, more specialized collections are the product of the enterprising Elgar Editions and contain both biographical and critical material, new and reprinted. One such volume commemorates the centenary of *The Dream of Gerontius* but has not, so far, been followed by centenary tributes to the other oratorios.[27] Elgar Editions has also produced a fascinating symposium of Elgar and the First World War, and published Robert Anderson's idiosyncratic study, *Elgar and Chivalry*.[28]

The last mentioned is a good example of the advantage gained by later writers from the biographical work of predecessors, including in this case Anderson himself. *Elgar and Chivalry* broadens and deepens areas of cultural exploration that seem at times to go right outside the composer's immediate preoccupations, but which form part of a world, and world view—his, and of those around him. In marked contrast to the chivalric theme, Byron Adams has embraced notions of 'decadence' contemporary to Elgar, of which the defining moment was the Oscar Wilde trial.[29] This further enlargement of what must be perceived as part of Elgar's cultural environment may not please everybody, but Adams's scholarship defines aspects of the period that cannot be ignored, and that, to be positive, rectify any image of the era as one of mainly nationalist tub-thumping. The music reflects its era, but also purposes it serves subsequently. The last night of the Proms, anticipated by use of the trio in the Coronation Ode, marks out the first *Pomp and Circumstance* march as a jingoistic fling; but its off-key introduction is only one of several compositional features within the collection of five (or six!) that is noteworthy for musical subtlety. Some passages in these marches are scarcely more bombastic than *Chanson de matin*.

One cannot hope to do justice to the wealth of material on Elgar now emerging from various publishers, and in journals both British and American; some continental scholars are reviving European interest in Elgar, whose rising stock abroad is probably attributable, once again, to the championship of his music by conductors, many of them not British. Meanwhile, and in anticipation of further delights and, one must hope, jolts to any residual complacency, we can digest the substantial monographs emerging from Cambridge University Press. J. P. E. Harper-Scott's is an intense music-analytic study informed by wide philosophical reading and deep contemplation.[30] Matthew Riley has prepared a book centred on a kind of post-Moore or scholarly pastoral, together with thorough examination of such themes as nostalgia and the loss of childhood—themes which by no means return Elgar to the English provinces. Both authors—like Diana McVeagh in her forthcoming study—engage closely with the actual notes, showing acute sensitivity to their interaction and significance. It is much to be regretted that competent musicians and lovers of music so often shrink from such close readings; some, at the word 'analysis', shy like a frightened horse. All analysis does is consider the interaction of purely musical elements, not necessarily at the expense of its intellectual and emotional content. It should be a welcome and exciting development when those who contribute to the discipline of music analysis and criticism add Elgar to their portfolio of composers studied: James Hepokoski, for instance, who has written influentially on Verdi, Strauss and Sibelius, or the Wagner scholar Patrick McCreless.[31]

In this short survey I have traced what appears to me to be a growing concern for the fullest possible understanding of the world in which Elgar lived and composed, coupled with a determination finally to come to grips with the music itself and its significance. Questions of meaning arise at every turn, and, without bemusing the reader by too many further citations, I have read with fascinated attention studies of music in most of the genres Elgar cultivated. Of music with words, songs and part-songs are admittedly less studied than the cantatas and oratorios.[32] Our understanding of instrumental music with a programme is happily being re-complicated, notably Elgar's tragic—yes, tragic—*Falstaff*; works with no overt programme, particularly, of course, the symphonies, are perceived as bearing complexities of meaning as well as musical form. While some may consider ill-advised the recent tendency towards wide-ranging investigation of cultural issues apparently peripheral to the job of musical composition, it has engendered more in the way of insight into the man Elgar and, especially, his music than any number of attempts to grasp the slippery, and in my view chimerical, mystery of the enigma of the *Variations*. As for that work, what matters remains its deserved status as Elgar's first metropolitan and international success, something best illuminated not by the dark glass of cryptography but by shining light upon it from biographical, cultural, and musical—including analytical —investigation.

Notes

1 W. H. Reed, *Elgar as I knew him* (London: Gollancz, 1936); *Elgar* (London: Dent, 1939)

2 Mrs R. Powell, *Edward Elgar: Memories of a Variation* (London: Oxford University Press, 1937; 2nd edition, 1947; 3rd revised edition, Aldershot: Scolars Press, 1994).

3 R. Burley and F. C. Carruthers, *Edward Elgar: The Record of a Friendship* (London: Barrie and Jenkins, 1972).

4 E. W. Atkins, *The Elgar-Atkins Friendship* (Newton Abbot: David and Charles, 1984).

5 D. McVeagh, *Edward Elgar: His Life and Music* (London: Dent, 1955); P. M. Young, *Elgar OM, A Study of a Musician* (London: Collins, 1955). Young also contributed to the genre of biography of composers' wives: *Alice Elgar: Enigma of a Victorian Lady* (London: Dobson, 1978).

6 D. McVeagh, *Elgar the Music Maker* (Woodbridge: Boydell and Brewer, 2007).

7 I. Parrott, *Elgar* (London: Dent, 1971).

8 R. Anderson, *Elgar* (London: Dent, 1993).

9 M. Kennedy, *A Portrait of Elgar* (London: Oxford University Press, 1968; revised second and third editions, 1973 and 1987).

10 See J. P. E. Harper-Scott, 'Elgar's deconstruction of the belle époque: interlace structures and the Second Symphony', in Harper-Scott and J. Rushton (eds), *Elgar Studies* (Cambridge University Press, 2007); *Elgar: an Extraordinary Life* (London: Associated Board of the Royal Schools of Music, 2007). See also B. Porter, *The Absent-Minded Imperialists: Empire, Society and Culture in Britain*

(New York: Oxford University Press, 2004) and 'Elgar and Empire: Music, Nationalism, and the War', in L. Foreman (ed.), *Oh, My Horses! Elgar and the Great War* (Rickmansworth: Elgar Editions, 2001), pp. 133–173.

11　Letter to A. J. Jaeger, 21 July 1898 in J. N. Moore (ed.), *Elgar and His Publishers: Letters of a Creative Life* (2 Vols, Oxford: Clarendon Press, 1987), p. 79.

12　Letter to Frances Colvin, 14 March 1912, in J. N. Moore (ed.) *Edward Elgar: Letters of a Lifetime* (Oxford: Clarendon Press, 1990), p. 244.

13　See for instance C. Gould, '"Behind thy veil close-drawn": Elgar, *The Crown of India*, and the feminine "other"', in R. Cowgill and J. Rushton (eds), *Europe, Empire, and Spectacle in Nineteenth-Century British Music* (Aldershot: Ashgate, 2006), pp. 210–219. My views on the unfortunate heritage of empire appear in 'Elgar, Kingdom, and Empire', *Elgar Society Journal* 14/6 (November 2006), 15–26.

14　N. G. Gwynne, 'Elephants and Moghuls, Contraltos and G-strings: how Elgar got his Englishness'.

15　M. Kennedy, *Portrait of Elgar; The Life of Elgar* (Cambridge: Cambridge University Press, 2004).

16　J. N. Moore, *Edward Elgar: A Creative Life* (London: Oxford University Press, 1984); *Elgar and His Publishers; Elgar: The Windflower Letters* (Oxford: The Clarendon Press, 1989); *Edward Elgar: Letters of a Lifetime*.

17　J. N. Moore, *Elgar: Child of Dreams* (London: Faber and Faber, 2004).

18　Moore (ed.), *Elgar and His Publishers*, p. 86.

19　See M. Kennedy, *Britten* (London: Dent, 1981), p. 113.

20　Letter to Jaeger, 9 March 1898 in Moore, *Elgar and His Publishers*, p. 69.

21　Moore, *A Creative Life*, p. 823.

22　R. Monk (ed.), *Elgar Studies* (Aldershot: Scolars Press, 1990).

23　R. Monk (ed.), *Edward Elgar: Music and Literature* (Aldershot: Scolars Press, 1993).

24　D. M. Grimley and J. Rushton (eds), *The Cambridge Companion to Elgar* (Cambridge: Cambridge University Press, 2004); Harper-Scott and Rushton (eds), *Elgar Studies*.

25　B. Adams (ed.), *Elgar and his World* (Princeton University Press, forthcoming).

26　C. Redwood (ed.), *An Elgar Companion* (Ashbourne: Sequoia Publishing, 1982).

27　G. Hodgkins (ed.), *The Best of Me: A Gerontius Centenary Companion* (Rickmansworth: Elgar Editions, 1999).

28　L. Foreman (ed.), *Oh, My Horses!* (see note 10 above); Robert Anderson, *Elgar and Chivalry* (Rickmansworth: Elgar Editions, 2002).

29　See B. Adams's essay on the oratorios in *The Cambridge Companion to Elgar*, and 'The "Dark Saying" of the Enigma: Homoeroticism and the Elgarian Paradox', *19th-Century Music*, 23 (2000) 218–35.

30　J. P. E. Harper-Scott, *Edward Elgar, Modernist* (Cambridge University Press, 2006); M. Riley, *Edward Elgar and the Nostalgic Imagination* (Cambridge University Press, 2007).

31　J. A. Hepokoski, 'Elgar', in D. Kern Holoman (ed.), *The Nineteenth-Century Symphony* (New York: Schirmer, 1997), pp. 327–44, an article often cited. Both McCreless and Hepokoski contribute essays to the forthcoming *Elgar Studies*.

32 See, for example, the work of C. E. McGuire: *Elgar's Oratorios: The Creation of an Epic Narrative* (Aldershot: Ashgate, 2002), an essay on *Caractacus* in *Elgar Studies*, and further consideration of Elgar's Roman Catholicism forthcoming in *Elgar and his World*.

3

A View From 1955

DIANA McVEAGH

In 1946 the Royal College of Music founded an essay prize in memory of H. C. Colles, who had studied and taught there and who had died in 1943. Colles had been chief music critic of *The Times* and editor of two editions of *Grove*. His successor on *The Times*, Frank Howes, whose pupil I was, persuaded me to enter the competition. I won (there were only three entries). The subject was 'Concerto: Contest or Cooperation?' and I made no mention of Elgar. The valuable part of the prize was publication in *Music & Letters*, edited by Eric Blom. In his letter acknowledging my returned proofs, Blom added a postscript: 'You wouldn't like to write a book on Elgar, would you?'

Poor Blom was scraping the barrel. Why else invite a 20-year-old girl student to write about one of the country's great composers? The book should have been written by W. McNaught of Novello, whose early, succinct and sympathetic paperback on Elgar is still good reading today. His father and Elgar had been friendly colleagues. But McNaught had hardly begun his task when he found that he had inoperable cancer. I did not realize till long after I had accepted the commission that Blom had approached two or three other writers before me, who had turned the proposition down. I was a last resort. Elgar, in the mid-twentieth century, was not thought a proper academic subject.

The 1914–18 war had so changed the cultural climate that in 1933 Constant Lambert could in write in *Music Ho!* that for his generation Elgar 'through no fault of his own' had 'an almost intolerable air of smugness, self-assurance and autocratic benevolence'. Stanford and Dent had made Cambridge uncomfortable for Elgarians. During the years of my book's preparation Percy Young also wrote his. In his preface he remarked, without actually admitting he had been up at Cambridge, 'I was tutored by those whose attitude to Elgar lacked enthusiasm—to say the least of it. When I admitted to one that *Gerontius* had overwhelmed me he said, "Ah! Yes—the first time. But wait, it won't happen again."' Jack Westrup at Oxford was more sympathetic, writing and lecturing several times on Elgar. Michael Kennedy, writing in 1990, spoke of the time twenty years previously as 'before the wider revival of interest in [Elgar's] music had gained full momentum'.

It had not always been like that. In Elgar's heyday he was taken up not only by Richter, who after all was living in this country. Nikisch, Steinbach, Walter, Weingartner all conducted his music before 1914. He was fêted in the United States, conducted his music there and in Canada, and was taken up by Theodore Thomas in Chicago, by Walter Damrosch in New York. Mahler conducted the *Enigma Variations* in New York in 1911. Kreisler premiered the Violin Concerto. But after two world wars it was left to the British local stalwarts, in particular Boult and Sargent, to carry the tradition to the younger conductors who in the last couple of decades have conducted and recorded Elgar faithfully and freshly, at home and abroad.

Elgar is not the only composer whose reputation has gone up and down. *Peter Grimes* in 1945 changed the face of English music, though for the 1951 Festival of Britain every choral society still wanted to sing *Gerontius*. The Festival commissioned works from William Alwyn, Gordon Jacob, Alan Rawsthorne and Edmund Rubbra (Bliss and Bax failed to produce their works). The competition for a new British opera was won by George Lloyd's *John Socman*. Peter Racine Fricker won the concerto competition. Lennox Berkeley, John Ireland and E. J. Moeran were repertory composers then. In the 1950s Handel was scarcely ever seen on the stage, at least in this country. Bellini and Donizetti were not deemed worth serious consideration. Mahler's and Bruckner's symphonies were rarities in our concert halls. Later familiarity with them challenged the received opinion that Elgar's symphonies were 'too long'. (Redlich's combined *Bruckner and Mahler* also came out in

1955, in Half-Master Musicians, as it were.) Rachmaninoff was thought too easily accessible to be quite proper. Sibelius was rated more highly, and played more often, then than now. In criticism, it was before the New Musicology, and reception history had not been heard of.

Of source books on Elgar there were Robert Buckley (1905) and Basil Maine (1933), both published during his lifetime and so to some extent with his cooperation. Ernest Newman (1906) and Thomas Dunhill (1938) covered the music only. The memoirs of 'Dorabella' and W. H. Reed, both enchanting books, had no scholarly pretensions. I regret so much that my youth, diffidence and inexperience meant that I did not ask Elgar's daughter as much as I could have done. I hesitated to intrude. Looking back, I believe she might have welcomed friendship. Meeting Dorabella, I marvelled at how this short, stoutish, forthright lady, with more than a hint of a moustache, could have been the charming mischievous girl who delighted and amused Elgar. Talking with her, I was soon as bewitched as he. She insisted that the 'five dots' of the Violin Concerto stood for Julia Worthington; she had been told so by Elgar's wife. (Biographers learn that not everything said even by their subject's nearest and dearest should always be taken at face value.) Ivor Atkins, understandably dismissing me as a tiresome student, gave me short shrift. Little did I realise he knew the secret of Helen Weaver. I could even have met Elgar's last love, Vera Hockman, who did not die until 1963, though in her last years she was sadly ill.

Those were the days of typewriters and carbon paper, breakable records and steel, even fibre, gramophone needles. There was not much chance to hear little-known Elgar. When my *Elgar* was published in 1955 I had never heard the pre-*Gerontius* cantatas. It was possible to hear *The Apostles* and *The Kingdom* under Sargent at the Royal Choral Society concerts, and *The Spirit of England* was performed annually near Armistice Day. Now devoted Elgarians can listen over and over again in their own homes to works that are hardly ever performed in London concert halls. Recording has changed everything. Even 'fun' compositions are available on disc, such as the Smoking Cantata Elgar tossed off to amuse a house party and surely never meant for the public. But he might have rejoiced. He was prescient enough to become one of the first great composers to leave a recorded legacy. Not only do his recordings show how he played his music on a particular day (works he recorded more than once differ strikingly) but, as Robert Philip has shown, they are valuable historical documents about general performing practice of his period.

It is extraordinary now to remember Elgar's birthplace cottage at Broadheath as it then was. It was like discovering the Sleeping Beauty. The caretaker in those days was not a curator, though she had the back-up of Elgar's daughter who lived across the lane. I opened a drawer of his desk and some of his letters fell out. I could have walked off with dozens (but didn't). I doubt whether they were catalogued. While I was researching, there were no more than half-a-dozen visitors a week. Petrol was still short, not everyone had cars, visits to stately homes had not become popular weekend outings. Readers of Lees-Milne's *Caves of Ice* will have an idea of what life was like when the National Trust was still recruiting its great houses, long before the days of English Heritage.

It was Elgar's wish that his birthplace should be his memorial, but it was his wife's far-sightedness, her instinct to preserve everything of her beloved Edu, that made her keep his letters and sketches. The great holdings of sketches and autographs at the British Library mean that scholars can trace in detail the stages of most of his compositions, as Robert Anderson has shown in *Elgar in Manuscript* (1990). And not only earnestly. Elgar's wicked drawings enliven many pages. Rough but vivid pen-and-ink sketches of the Apostles (unflattering) and of Queen Victoria (not amused) in scrapbooks belonging to Elgar's nieces suggest that had he not been a musician he might have earned his keep as a cartoonist. (Recently, working on Gerald Finzi, how often I deplored his tidiness, his habit of destroying his sketches once a work was finished! But Finzi did keep letters.) The publication of Elgar's letters, expertly edited by Moore, has been of enormous importance. Apart from their sheer information, they show how differently he wrote to different friends, how one brought out the jocular, teasing, high-spirited side of him, another the despondent and introspective side. They show too his volatility, his violent mood swings, so that letters even written closely together suggest opposing emotions. Was his the last but one generation of creative artists to write and keep letters? There are great correspondences of, among others, Mahler, Delius, Strauss, and later Britten. How much are emails and mobile phones losing for future biographers?

Percy Young's book and mine came out the same week, so causing a little stir. The *Listener* review began 'The appearance of two books about Edward Elgar at a time when his music seems to be entering an eclipse suggests that if an eclipse is in the offing it will be only temporary.' Ernest Newman was prompted to write three important articles in *The Sunday Times*. He was the first to suggest some deep hidden emotion in Three Stars, variation XIII of 'Enigma'. He also described a visit to Elgar a few days before he died. Elgar spoke 'despondently of his fear that his music would not live after him'. Newman reassured him. Then Elgar 'made a simple short remark about himself . . . that explains a good deal', that had 'a particular bearing . . . on that passion of his for public mystification', his 'enigma' of the *Variations* and of the Soul of the Violin Concerto. Not that he disclosed their identity, Newman wrote, but the remark threw a light on the 'curious mentality that made mystification' necessary to him. It has always puzzled me that Elgar, having grown impatient with his friends trying to solve the enigma, should then invite speculation, intrusion into his privacy, with the five dots of the Concerto. It has even been suggested recently that the Elgars were their own 'spin doctors', knowingly manipulating the press for publicity. Newman refused to divulge what Elgar had said.

My book was commissioned (though in the end it was published separately) for the Master Musicians series, which in those days rigidly separated Life and Works. Since then biography has been radically changed, by Michael Holroyd on Lytton Strachey and Leon Edel on Henry James; and by writers such as Frances Spalding, Victoria Glendinning, Hilary Spurling, whose biographies read as compulsively as novels. A particular value of Moore's great study of Elgar (1984) is his integration of the life and music, the insight it gives into the day-to-day life of a composer, showing how proofs and performances of one work always overlap composition of the next.

Elgar's reputation, more than that of most composers, has been affected by extra-musical considerations. Because he composed marches called *Imperial, Empire, Coronation, Pomp and Circumstance*, he has been both revered as patriotic and denigrated as imperialist and jingoistic. He came to maturity at the zenith of the British Empire. Reaction against the period's excesses made for reaction against Elgar. Nothing shows the change more than what has happened to *The Spirit of England*. Composed during the 1914–1918 War, it caught the mood of that time. Today people who know it bewail its neglect. It might seem that Elgar and the pacifist Britten had little in common. Yet Britten admired its third movement, 'For the Fallen', for the 'agony of distortion' in its march, for its 'personal tenderness and grief' and its 'ring of genuine splendour'. The finest recording of Elgar's Introduction and Allegro (sadly, he did not record it himself) is that conducted by Britten.

4

Elgar the Catholic

STEPHEN HOUGH

M.E.

He quickly swung his wiry legs under the keyboard, attached his feet to the pedals, and cried out: 'What's this?' Twelve slow, ringing, sonorous chords trembled from within the piano and then bounced off the peeling walls of the teaching studio. 'I don't know, Mr Steele.' 'It's from *The Dream of Gerontius*, dear boy, by Sir Edward Elgar.' He began to play the chords again, now singing along with quavering emotion: '*Proficiscere, anima Christiana* . . . Go forth upon thy journey, Christian soul.' I, the student, was about 13 years old, the teacher was Douglas Steele, and the peeling walls were in Chetham's School in Manchester. I left that lesson in a daze, went as soon as I could to buy the score and records of the work, and then plunged into studying it as if into a baptism of total immersion. Little by little the words, as well as the music, began to fascinate me, an enthusiastically Evangelical teenager with a floppy, well-worn King James Bible. What was all this about saints, prayers for the dead, and Purgatory? Who was this Cardinal Newman? What on earth would make him *choose* to become a Roman Catholic? It took me three years or so before I began attending Mass and became a Catholic myself, but those twelve majestic chords were a literal exhortation to go forth upon a journey—one of music and of faith which continues to the present day.

England

If *The Dream of Gerontius* was my first step on the road towards Catholic faith it almost appears to have been Elgar's first step away from it. To begin to understand this we need to start by looking at the English Catholic world into which Elgar was born and we need to look at the man who wrote the words that Elgar set.

To make utterly simple an enormously complex subject, after the sixteenth-century Reformation, Roman Catholicism was outlawed in England. Although the actual persecutions became less severe and more rare as the years passed—the demand for someone to be hanged, drawn and quartered relaxed into a demand for their pounds, shillings and pence—it was not until 1778 that the law itself began to change, culminating in the Catholic Emancipation Act of 1829 which finally gave freedom to Catholics as regards worship, land ownership and employment.[1] At the time of emancipation, Catholics in England were basically divided into two different groups: the old aristocratic, recusant families whose wealth and pedigree had enabled them to hold on to their Catholicism beyond the Reformation and who lived their eccentric, isolated lives on vast country estates; and the working-class labourers, mainly Irish, who lived in pitiful squalor in the urban slums created by the Industrial Revolution. It was not really until after John Henry Newman's conversion to Rome in 1845, followed by a steady stream of imitators, and the re-establishment of the Catholic hierarchy in 1850, with its confident building of new churches across the land, that any sort of unified Catholic community began to come into existence. The converts eventually created a middle ground which, because of the diversity of their social background, served to 'normalize' Catholicism and to weave it gradually into the fabric of society, especially through mixed marriages, despite the serious tensions these could often engender.

Yet tensions were not limited to the Protestant–Catholic divide. The Catholic recusants had learned, over many centuries of persecution, to keep a low religious profile. They were happy just to be able to go to Mass on Sundays and Feast-days, and they found any kind of proselytizing of a faith so recently illegal to be vulgar, risky and embarrassing. This old guard had become known in the late eighteenth century as 'Cisalpines', meaning 'this side of the Alps'—an indication that they wanted to emphasize their loyalty to the British state and their opposition to Papal influence except in matters of doctrine. The new converts, on the other hand, would not rest until England was a Catholic country again, a politically explosive stance during those most imperialistic years of the second half of the nineteenth century. Roman catechisms of the time blustered: 'Those who are not in communion with the Bishop of Rome are either heretics or infidels.' The converts were not just noisy and enthusiastic, they were *converts*—the new kids on the block, the Johnny-come-latelies; and, despite genuine spiritual convictions, they seem also to have relished the whiff of scandal which such a counter-cultural move could generate.

If the converts' religious zeal alienated the gentry, their recurrent political conservatism made them few friends amongst the Irish workers, whose longing for Home Rule across the Irish Sea had to wait until 1922 to reach fulfilment, and who suffered their exile from famine and political injustice with no little resentment. Furthermore, the converts' frequent love of Roman trappings —richly decorated vestments, incense and high liturgy—could seem an eccentric pose to those who struggled to put the plainest clothes on their backs, to avoid the foulest stenches from filling their rooms, or to observe the wearying rituals of looking after their many children.

Elgar, for his part, had neither the glamour of the convert, the blue blood of the recusant, nor the camaraderie of the Catholic working-class communities with their large families. He was the son and husband of two converts, but his own cradle-Catholicism was ordinary at best, distasteful at worst, in a country which deeply distrusted 'Papists' and often referred to the Church of Rome as 'the Whore of Babylon'.

J. H. N.

'If only the Catholics were all that they ought to be!!! But there is too much egoism; too much politics and too little charity.' Thus wrote the Passionist priest Blessed Dominic Barberi in 1842, three years before he received Newman into the Catholic Church. He is a more important figure in this story than is generally realized, because he represented the gentle spirit of Catholicism which enabled Newman to overcome his hesitation and make the final decision to convert. Dominic's appearance in the grim, industrial Midlands in his worn sandals, his torn, black Passionist habit clinking with rosary beads, his warm hug and smile, and his appalling, broken English, was like a shaft of Italian sun breaking through the clouds. John Henry Newman was one of the most celebrated Anglican priests and intellectuals of his day. His gradual discovery of a more Catholic understanding of Christianity through his study of history and of early Church writings led him first of all to be involved in the founding of the Oxford Movement and then to leap over the Tiber into the heart of Rome. It is hard for us in the twenty-first century to realize quite what a shock this move would have been, not just to the establishment of the Established Church, but also to a large majority of ordinary English people. It would have seemed an act of treason, of apostasy, of intellectual suicide, of bad social taste . . . indeed, almost of insanity.[2] One of the reasons Newman found the move to Rome so difficult was that it was a profound social as well as theological change. Not only were all of his friends members of the Church of England, but he had little in common with those to whom he would be sent as a newly minted Catholic priest. This became a key factor in his choice to found an oratory[3] rather than to join an established religious order or diocese. He was able to create a kind of Oxford club in the Edgbaston suburb of Birmingham, gathering like-minded and like-tasted brothers around him. Even chamber music was a regular feature of their fraternal evenings, and Newman was a keen violinist. Although Newman's life as a Roman Catholic was not easy—he was often the subject of suspicion and calumny—he had a profound influence on Catholic life in England and abroad during his lifetime and well into the twentieth century. The Second Vatican Council (1962–5) has often been called 'Newman's Council' in recognition of his spirit hovering over some of its ideas and teachings.[4]

E. E.

The external facts of Elgar's Catholic life are straightforward enough. It all began, appropriately, with St George, the patron saint of England; and, more specifically, with the Catholic church which bears his name in Worcester. In 1846 William Elgar, a musical man-about-town who ran the music shop and tuned pianos, took the job as organist at St George's, and in 1848 married Anne Greening. In 1852, after accompanying her husband to church regularly on Sundays, she decided to convert to Catholicism, although William remained an agnostic until his deathbed conversion. In 1857 Edward was born and was baptized at St George's. From 1863 to 1872 he attended small Catholic schools in the area where the education was good but probably quite narrow. He left school aged fifteen and began to assist his father at St George's, arranging and writing music for the choir. Worcester Cathedral was close by and he often attended services and concerts there, even though this would have been discouraged by Catholic discipline at the time. In 1879 he read Emile Zola's novel *L'Assommoir*, published two years earlier, and gave its title to a set of five quadrilles he had written. This would be of no special interest except that all of Zola's writings were to end up on the Vatican's Index of Forbidden Books by 1898, and he would certainly have been under suspicion when Elgar was reading him. Perhaps we see here already a certain spirit of independence from the traditional views which Elgar would have received in his education at school and church. In 1885 he took over the post of organist at St George's, and in 1886 he began to give lessons to Alice Roberts. In 1887 Alice's mother died and Elgar lent her his well-worn and annotated copy of a favourite poem, *The Dream of Gerontius* by Newman. In 1888 Elgar became engaged to Alice, to the outrage of her well-to-do relatives. One of her aunts actually wrote her out of her will in objection to her association with this penniless musician, the son of a tradesman and a Roman Catholic. They married at the Brompton Oratory[5] in 1889 in a Catholic ceremony but not a Nuptial Mass, as Alice was still a Protestant and would not have been able to take communion. In 1890 their only daughter, Carice, was born and was baptized at

Brook Green. In 1893 Alice was received into the Catholic Church at St George's in Worcester.

Age 43—Opus 38

To move to examine the internal Catholic life of Elgar (and its apparent collapse) is as problematic as it would be to look inside anyone's soul. He did not talk very much about his personal faith or lack of it, but we can gather a few clues from some of his letters and from the background to his most Catholic work.

In 1892, in a touching letter Elgar wrote to the children of some friends during a Bavarian holiday, he had taken up a third of the text enthusing about the folk-Catholicism he found there:

> No Protestants . . . church open all day . . . workmen carrying their rosaries . . . bells ringing at the elevation [in the Mass] at which people in the streets take off their hats and make the sign of the Cross . . . crucifixes on the roadsides . . . stations of the Cross . . . chapels to the blessed virgin . . . [6]

By 1899 he had had his first major success with the *Variations on an Original Theme* Op. 36. Each of its movements had been headed with the 'enigma' of some initials representing the names of his closest friends. His next large-scale work, the choral masterpiece *The Dream of Gerontius* Op. 38, had just one set of bold letters at its head: A.M.D.G. (*Ad Majoriam Dei Gloriam*).[7]

Curiously, Dvořák had been invited by the Birmingham Festival in the late 1880s to set Newman's poem to music, but it was eventually deemed to be too controversial and he wrote his Requiem instead. When Elgar was commissioned by the same festival in 1900, he suggested the same text—a daringly provocative gesture, and a significant risk for a young English composer receiving his first important commission on the back of his first big success. England was a deeply Protestant country, and such a subject choice would be a little like selecting a Talmudic text for an Islamic festival commission.[8] Yet Elgar went ahead with total disregard for any possible censure or disfavour, making it hard to believe that the words had no religious meaning for him at the time, especially as he was aware, and had complained, that his faith was an impediment to his career. At the suggestion by his publisher Jaeger that there was too much 'Joseph and Mary' about the work, he replied:

> Of course it will frighten the low church party but the poem must on no account be touched! Sacrilege and not to be thought of . . . It's awfully curious the attitude (towards sacred things) of the narrow English mind.

And again to Jaeger he wrote: 'I have written my heart's blood into the score . . . I have written out my insidest inside.' When he gave the original manuscript of the full score as a gift to the Birmingham Oratory he wrote to Fr Bellasis: 'I must add that nothing would give me greater happiness than to feel that the work into which I put my whole soul should be in its original form, near to where the sacred author of the poem made his influence felt.'

Yet only weeks after its disastrous premiere he would write to Jaeger:

> Providence denies me a decent hearing of my work: so I submit—I always said God was against art & I still believe it . . . I have allowed my heart to open once—it is now shut against every religious feeling & every soft, gentle impulse for ever.

Although this sounds more like a temper tantrum than a reasoned rebellion against belief, it does suggest that his Catholicism was not deep-rooted and was more cultural than credal. It also appears to mark the beginning of a steady walk away from the Church, and of an increasingly black, depressive mood that would overshadow his emotional life until the end. The death of his mother in 1902—the woman who had first brought Catholicism into the family and who had been his comfort and solace during earlier times of crisis —might have made it easier for him to express his religious doubts more openly as the years passed. Although after reading Shaw's *Man and Superman* in 1904 he could still write to Arthur Troyte Griffith:

Bernard Shaw is hopelessly wrong, as all these fellows are, on
fundamental things:—amongst others they punch Xtianity & try
to make it fit their civilization instead of making their civilization
fit It;

nevertheless, revealing references continue to pop up in letters
mentioning Alice or Carice being at church whilst he remained at
home. For a Catholic to miss Mass on Sunday deliberately was
considered a mortal sin, and to do so was a clear sign that Elgar's
institutional faith was nominal.

Explaining a person's move away from belief (or, for that matter,
towards belief) is ultimately impossible. An event which destroys
one person's faith (an illness, the death of a loved one) can re-ignite
another's. Success and happiness can open one's heart to God with
joy and gratitude, or they can make Him seem superfluous and
extraneous to a busy, fulfilled life. We only know what a person
tells us, and Elgar's petty rant against God to Jaeger quoted above,
reflecting more on his mood than on his mind, could never have
been enough to tip the balance; but I think there is a telltale clue in
his use of the word 'Providence': a view of God as Fate rather than
Father. In addition, his search for lost innocence, about which
Michael Kennedy writes,[9] is a further, false Christian vision. Such a
search is always for *our* innocence—a vague phantom from some
distant past that never really existed. Christianity's essence is the
discovery in the present that such an innocence does not actually
matter; it has been replaced by the innocence of Christ as a gift to
be received, not searched for.

The Coming (and Departing) of the Kingdom

Elgar's next big choral work after *Gerontius* was written as a result
of a commission from the 1903 Birmingham Festival, and it has
been suggested by Byron Adams[10] that the research Elgar under-
took in the composition of *The Apostles* (and, later, *The Kingdom*)
might have been an element in the unsettling of his faith. He read
many modern scripture scholars and consulted two Anglican
clergymen,[11] and it is certain that some of the books on Elgar's desk
would also have been on the Vatican's Index. Catholic biblical

scholarship at the time lagged far behind, and erroneous teachings such as the single authorship by Moses of the first five books of the Bible, St Paul's authorship of the Letter to the Hebrews, and the authenticity of the extra verses in chapter five of the First Letter of St John were only to be challenged under pain of sin. An increasing siege mentality had taken hold after the dismantling of the Papal States in 1870 left the Pope a 'prisoner' in the Apostolic Palace in the Vatican,[12] and by the early years of the twentieth century a witch-hunt of theologians and priests suspected of Modernism was taking place. Indeed, London was an important centre in this controversy as two of the key 'villains' lived and worked there—Fr George Tyrrell[13] and Baron Friedrich von Hügel. Elgar could not fail to have been aware of these controversies, and his research at the time could well have led him to distrust the absolute veracity of certain Catholic doctrine.

In later life Elgar's move away from religious belief seems to have been even more determined. To George Bernard Shaw, with whom he established a fond friendship, he was reputed to have wished that the 'nots' of the commandments could be inserted into the creed; and on his deathbed he refused to see a priest and asked for his cremated[14] ashes to be scattered by a favourite river rather than receive a Catholic burial. Yet frustration regarding the commandments and creed could be seen in some ways as a Christian reflex. Christ himself removed some 'nots' from the commandments of his time and manifested a great intolerance of unnecessary rules and laws which he described as heavy burdens on people's backs which religious leaders refused to help lift. Some Catholic Canon Law can be at least as complex and arcane as anything condemned by Christ in the Gospels; and the quip, 'The Italians make the rules, the Irish keep them' is a rueful reflection on the state of scrupulosity which had made its way into the bloodstream of Christianity, especially in the Northern countries—amongst both Catholics and Protestants. This way of thinking created a religious atmosphere, a repressive and reactionary fog, with which someone of Elgar's background and generation would have been all too familiar.

There was a period after Elgar's death when some Elgarians, notably Sir Adrian Boult, professed to prefer *The Kingdom* to

Gerontius, and one wonders whether this was purely on musical grounds. Certainly the average Englishman in the first half of the twentieth century would have found its clean-cut 'Churchiness' much more to his taste than the *Dream*'s agony and ecstasy. But I have a feeling that today this is a shrinking group. It is not just that the narrative sweep of Newman's poem gives *Gerontius* a dramatic shape which is lacking in the set-piece tableaux of the two biblical oratorios; but the inner drama of creative conviction seems to be missing too. The Catholic candles and incense have been removed, but so too has the flame which set them alight in the first place. Much has been written in speculation as to why Elgar did not finish his projected trilogy of 'apostolic' oratorios. Although it is clear he wanted to write a symphony and to explore more abstract forms, this is not reason enough. It is surely more likely that he simply lost interest in a subject about which he could only write music from his heart or not at all. *Gerontius* is carried along with the fervour of faith, flushed with the pride of identity and belonging. But by the middle years of the Edwardian reign Elgar's passions had found new creative outlets: regret at the disappearance of the Victorian England and its culture which he loved, and a new, engrossing attachment to a new Alice—Lady Alice Stuart-Wortley.[15] These were to inspire the works written after he reluctantly, and agonizingly, managed to put the finishing touches to *The Kingdom* in 1906.[16] Ironically the final 'touch' was probably to write at the top of the score those same letters, A.M.D.G., which had been chosen for *Gerontius*. Was this merely a formula by now, or the flickering, dying embers of faith? Whichever, it remains an enigma that only the composer could solve.

J. H. N. Again

It is intriguing that Elgar suggested St Augustine as one of the possible topics for the 1900 Birmingham Festival commission which eventually became *The Dream of Gerontius*. It was rejected as too controversial—strange, for a universally accepted Father of the Church and uncle of the Reformation. Martin Luther, John Calvin and Newman all felt more at home with the clean, black and white tones of Augustine than they did with the warmer, more complex palette of St Thomas Aquinas.

There was a reflex of Puritanism present in Newman from his earliest Christian life which never fully left him. Contemporary Catholics such as Cardinal Manning[17] and Fr Faber, and many others since, have sensed a certain coldness and lack of joy in Newman. His famous moodiness and touchiness with people, and his distaste at the 'smell' of some of his poor parishioners (he may not have found the piano tuner's son too congenial!) is a far cry from the carefree abandon of Dominic Barberi or other great Catholic saints. His giving up of pleasure can seem like a distrust of it rather than a way to celebrate its goodness by a generous donation; and even in his theology there is sometimes a mean-spirited view of God and salvation. When Gerontius asks the angel why, after being afraid of death whilst on earth, he is now not afraid of the Judgment, he is told, 'It is because then thou didst fear that now thou dost not fear. Thou hast forestalled the agony.' What sort of divine logic is involved in such a contorted thesis? And if that seems suspect, the following extract from an early sermon, delivered when he was still an Anglican, but still in print in his Catholic years, deserves condemnation as heresy:

> We should remember that [this life] is scarcely more than an accident of our being—that it is no part of ourselves, who are immortal spirits, independent of time and space . . . We should consider . . . life to be a sort of dream, as detached and as different from our real eternal existence as a dream differs from waking; a serious dream, indeed, as affording a means of judging us, yet in itself a kind of shadow without substance.[18]

This is not Christianity, and not Catholicism. Its dismissal of the material world is infected with a dualistic way of thinking about spirit and flesh which has been a constant threat to spiritual health throughout Christian history; and it is the very opposite of a faith whose foundation is God taking flesh in Christ and thereby sanctifying all things human.

Although *Gerontius* is not as un-Catholic as that, a case could be made that it has elements in it of the acquired Catholicism of a convert—a new suit not quite worn-in. Newman's God can seem a distant figure to be feared, a Victorian father of justice and righteousness, but of little warmth. In St Luke's Gospel[19] the Good Thief is assured by the Son of God that he will be with him in Paradise that very day; Gerontius has to make do with a mere angel telling him to be patient! The parable of the Prodigal Son[20] is the *news*, the Good News, of God as Father, rushing out to meet his half-repentant son, not even wanting to hear his fumbled, almost insincere words of contrition, but rather holding a great party of celebration at his safe return. (I wonder if the very joy of the father's forgiving and forgetting was what actually melted the son's heart to repentance; before that he appears to be returning home just for food and shelter.) There is no party in Newman's *Gerontius*, and, for all the glorious moments of universal faith which radiate from its pages, its 'dream' is ultimately shaped by Oxford spires and the draughty, damp, dusty corridors of mid-nineteenth-century English presbyteries where death was quietly endured behind wax-polished doors. And it was behind those same doors, in school and church, that Elgar first learned his catechism.

The Outsider

Elgar's Catholicism is central to understanding his music: not because, like Messiaen, it was the principal subject matter, but because it created the internal tensions and frictions out of which flowed a profusion of deeply personal musical ideas. Whether through his struggle with its religious or moral teachings, or because it was the locks on the doors which otherwise might have opened to professional or social acceptance, it is the backdrop to every scene in his creative life. It became the symbol for him of being an outsider; it was the 'pain' he could put his finger on, the scapegoat always there to receive his resentment at any perceived lack of success, of recognition, of honour. Perhaps he was not totally paranoid in this, as Charles Villiers Stanford and Cecil Forsyth's *History of Music*, published in 1917, describes him as follows:

Cut off from his contemporaries by the circumstances of his religion and his want of regular academic training, he was lucky enough to enter the field and find the preliminary ploughing already done.

However much this represents the jealousy of less-talented colleagues, it underlines the anti-Catholicism which was still part of English life at the time.

As an aside, it is interesting to compare Elgar's sense of being a social outsider with his exact contemporary, H. G. Wells. Their backgrounds were similar—both sons of tradesmen—but they took opposite positions on almost every subject. Wells found a confident, modern voice in new scientific advances, whereas Elgar disliked the encroaching modern world. Wells thrived in urban and suburban settings, whereas Elgar was unhappy away from the countryside. Wells embraced his atheism with no qualms, whereas Elgar never quite managed to leave behind his childhood Catholicism. Wells used his lower social standing and disadvantaged start as a spur to achievement, writing autobiographical novels such as *Kipps* and *The History of Mr Polly* in celebration of his humble beginnings; whereas Elgar resented his background and tried to overcome its taint by becoming part of the establishment and writing works for the Royal Family. Wells was a social prophet whereas Elgar was uncomfortable with new fashions and mores. Wells had public extra-marital affairs, whereas Elgar was tortured with crushes and half-fulfilled longings: the freethinking, modern man versus the doubting, country squire. Yet they are both archetypal men of their time, emerging out of the fractured egg of Victorianism: one waddling confidently away, the other looking ruefully at the broken shell.

Second Spring

Michael Kennedy has made the point[21] that *The Dream of Gerontius* is really a work from the last year of the nineteenth century. So, from the viewpoint of the twenty-first century, I wonder if Elgar might have been more at home living now than he was in his own times. To begin with, he is loved and appreciated today as never before; books and recordings abound, and he is performed wherever classical music is heard. His need to be accepted by a fossilized system of privilege and class would be irrelevant now. The rise from shopkeeper to knight is not at all uncommon, and today's House of Lords (whilst it lasts) comprises people from all walks of life —including even women! His religion, in our multi-cultural society, would not be the handicap it was; and I think Elgar would feel more at ease in a Catholic Church which is more open to the world outside, and less harsh with those inside whose faith is weak or wavering. Since the Second Vatican Council many of the 'nots' (and knots) of Church commandments and rules have been done away with—Friday fasting, the forbidding of worship with non-Catholics, and countless other liturgical and ecclesiastical laws. In addition, Elgar's sympathy with the character of Judas (he started to write an essay about him) is mirrored in some twenty-first-century theological debates. The composer realized instinctively that an over-narrow application of the doctrine of predestination in the case of this disciple struck a 'shattering blow' at faith, a line of reasoning with which the present Pope and Archbishop of Canterbury would have both sympathy and insight.

The musical life of Britain is now unarguably in the front rank in every way, and this would have been a tremendous encouragement to Elgar. The development of recording techniques (a medium for which he was extremely enthusiastic, making more recordings than any composer of his time) would have delighted him, and his love of tinkering about in his shed with chemical and mechanical experiments would surely today have led to him acquiring many modern gadgets and a high-speed broadband connection. As a keen bicycler he would have approved heartily of the interest in cycling the world over, with special lanes, grids in which to park, not to mention foldable models which he could have taken on train journeys into the deepest countryside. He loved visiting Italy and enjoyed his experience flying to France in 1933; it is not hard to imagine him taking regular trips abroad with great gusto. The founding of the RSPCA[22] after the Second World War would have made him extremely happy, as he provocatively claimed to prefer animals to humans. And finally, for the modest son of a shopkeeper, how could he fail to be tickled pink by the fact that his face now appears in countless millions of shops, banks, casinos and wallets across the world, on the back of every English twenty-pound note!

Notes

1 Other quirks remained—for example it was not until 1871 that Catholics were allowed to attend Oxford or Cambridge Universities; and, as I write this, the monarch of the United Kingdom can be a Confucian, but not a Catholic.

2 It is worth noting that this was a time when Blessed Dominic was often stoned as he walked along the road to say Mass.

3 The Congregation of the Oratory was founded by St Philip Neri (1515–1595) in Rome, and its innovative, non-liturgical services, with their fine music, were the beginnings of what became the oratorio. In addition, Philip was a close friend of both Palestrina and Victoria.

4 Interestingly, James Joyce, in *The Portrait of the Artist as a Young Man*, puts into the mouth of his literary *alter ego*, Stephen Dedalus, the opinion that Newman was the greatest writer of prose in the English language.

5 Founded by Fr Frederick William Faber, Newman's fellow convert, Oratorian, and often bitter rival.

6 All ellipses and square brackets mine.

7 To the Greater Glory of God—coincidentally the motto of the Jesuit order who ran St George's when Elgar was there.

8 The prejudice against the text of *Gerontius* continued for many years, and some performances were only allowed with alterations. Indeed, as recently as the 1990s there were letters of complaint written to a newspaper in Indianapolis when their Symphony was performing the work, objecting to the overtly Catholic nature of the text.

9 M. Kennedy, *The Life of Elgar* (Cambridge: Cambridge University Press, 2004).

10 In B. Adams, 'Elgar's Later Oratorios' in D. M. Grimley and J. Rushton (eds), *The Cambridge Companion to Elgar* (Cambridge: Cambridge University Press, 2004).

11 Edward Capel-Cure and Charles Gorton.

12 The doctrine of Papal Infallibility was defined in that same year at the First Vatican Council, perhaps to insist on the unchanging spiritual power remaining at the heart of the Church at the very moment when temporal power had been lost.

13 Dismissed from the Jesuit order in 1906 after trying in his writings to reconcile Catholic teaching with elements of contemporary philosophy.

14 Cremation was forbidden for Catholics until 1963.

15 'Windflower', as Elgar nicknamed her. She and the composer had a passionate, but almost certainly unconsummated, relationship until Elgar's death, and such a dangerous liaison cannot have helped his relationship with the Church.

16 Lady Elgar's diaries talk of a black depression in this period, and there are oblique references to suicidal thoughts.

17 Henry Edward Manning, Archbishop of Westminster from 1865 to 1892—also a convert.

18 J. H. Newman, *Parochial and Plain Sermons* Vol. 14 no. 4. Longman, 1890.

19 Lk. 23.43

20 Lk. 15.11–32

21 M. Kennedy, 'After 100 Years' in G. Hodgkins (ed.), *The Best of Me: A Gerontius Centenary Companion* (Rickmansworth: Elgar Editions, 1999).

22 Royal Society for the Prevention of Cruelty to Animals.

Part 2: Elgar the Composer

5

Elgar in Manuscript

ROBERT ANDERSON

Elgar at work inspires profound respect. His progress through various experiences of amateur music-making to the conductor's podium, whether in a lunatic asylum or at the Albert Hall, gave him sure knowledge not only of how to write for the orchestra but also how to nurse orchestral players towards perfect confidence in his scores. Many a performance has been saved by his meticulous insistence on adequate cues in orchestral parts, and the precision of his expression marks (including metronome timings) means much of the conductor's work is done even before the first down-beat. In this he is at the opposite extreme from a composer such as Delius, who needed a genius conductor to sort him out and insisted that Beecham's markings should be an integral part of his published music. Elgar achieved such certainty that a miniature score might appear before the premiere. Only at the keyboard was his instinct unsure. Even as late as the 1919 Piano Quintet he was suggesting Harold Brooke at Novello might add some pedal marks to the Adagio, if he yearned for them.

Elgar's hand changed remarkably during his working life. The neat jottings of the early sketch books that began in 1878, almost fussy in their precision, gradually give place to the bold sweep and assurance of later years. Indeed some late letters seem to have been penned as fast as thought, so characteristic is a style that takes some getting used to before transcription is sure. He would rather not use a fountain pen, preferring the constant dipping for ink to avoid cramp. His desk and materials can be examined at the Elgar Birthplace Museum. It is as well to remember that Elgar was also a consummate letter-writer in a large corpus that reflects his varying moods, whether playful, confident or self-piteous. To 'Nimrod' at Novello, a main emotional support till his early death in 1906, he gave detailed tidings of work in progress and wrote vigorous letters of protest about suggested additions to the *Enigma Variations* and *The Dream of Gerontius*, though finally if grudgingly admitting Jaeger was right.

Perhaps the most striking example of Elgar's virtuosity as both composer and letter-writer occurs in July 1908, when he was busy knocking the First Symphony into shape, 'working at speed' or 'very hard', as Lady Elgar commented in her diary. It was then he sent notes on the *Wand of Youth* Suite No. 2 to F. G. Edwards, editor of *The Musical Times*. Edwards happened to live at Potters Bar, a name that inspired Elgar to theories each more fantastic than the last: 'Who was Potter & why did he possess a Bar? Surely he did not keep a pub or act as a sedentary highwayman at a private "pike".' He must have been a philosopher, faced 'with some impenetrable riddle before which the mighty intellect—even that of Potter—quailed, paled & failed. Surely this was Potter's Bar.' A bar of soap or indeed of music was out of the question. Likewise, heraldry was little help. Of course Potter was 'acutely English', so the French 'barre' would have to become 'Potter's Bend'.

Self-taught, Elgar was systematic in his musical instruction. It took him no time to decide he had no place in a lawyer's office. There was his father's music shop in Worcester High Street, source for knowledge of the current repertoire. At the Birthplace Museum are the primers he studied, interlarded with characteristic comments of approval or the reverse. His father was organist at St George's Roman Catholic church. The young Elgar deputized for him occasionally; but more important was the nearby Cathedral, where he would scurry to hear the concluding voluntary after Matins, and where he became proficient enough on the violin to play in the Three Choirs Festivals. Early products for the church included a Gloria that pasted Elgarian choral parts over the violin line of the second movement in Mozart's F major Sonata K547, and a Credo that cobbled a credible work from Beethoven symphonies, the start of No. 5, Allegretto of No. 7 and slow movement of No. 9.

Early sketchbooks are full of incomplete works, some of the most promising embryo string quartets. Elgar needed the stimulus of a commission and discipline of a deadline throughout his life, and it is characteristic that some of the string music turned into wind quintets, an ensemble of which he was the bassoonist and which met regularly enough to require a constant supply of new music. These 'Shed' works show Elgar coming to terms with the Viennese Classics if not his own personality. Schumann was an early ideal, and his admiration for Wagner was clinched at a Crystal Palace memorial concert on 3 March 1883. On his programme he noted of the *Tristan* Prelude and 'Liebestod', 'I shall never forget this.' Certainly of equal importance was his marriage to Caroline Alice Roberts on 8 May 1889, daughter of an Indian Army major-general, and with the strength of character to make up for the tendency to procrastination Elgar probably inherited from his lackadaisical father.

At once she was part of the composing process. A first attempt at *The Black Knight* is ascribed to 'C. Alice & Edward Elgar', and in connection with the Op. 20 Serenade for Strings Elgar affirms that 'Braut helped a great deal to make these little tunes.' Her routine assistance was acknowledged on a *Bavarian Highlands* sketch: 'Koppid by Braut'; and till the end of her days she saved him hours of drudgery by laying out the pages of a full score once the instruments involved had been specified. Her belief in him was a paramount inspiration. How essential this was is clear from a *Black Knight* draft. It is headed '(proposed!) Ballad for Chorus & Orchestra', with the additional note of self-doubt, 'Music by Edward Elgar if he can'. The first three scenes were given to Novello on 23 July 1892, and the Elgars went on to Bayreuth for *Tristan*, *Die Meistersinger* and two performances of *Parsifal*. Wagner had taken real hold, so that he proposed the end of *The Black Knight* should be 'immer schwacher und schwacher'.

The *Black Knight* keyboard part was typical of Elgar's practice throughout his life. A competent pianist, he always drafted a work so that the two hands of a good amateur could encompass what he had written. So all his major choral pieces down to the wartime *Spirit of England* have piano parts by Elgar himself, though not acknowledged as such. And on vocal-score proofs he would mark off full-score pages as he started them. It was the same with orchestral works until the two symphonies. So the keyboard version of the *Enigma Variations* is in a sense the original. It was published separately and formed a working basis for the full score. The case of the symphonies is different (their arrangements are by Sigfrid Karg-Elert), since by then Elgar's mastery was such he did not need a complete blueprint before scoring. The *Falstaff* background material is even more sketchy. With the Cello Concerto Elgar needed a rough keyboard part for the soloist. It so happens he marked a couple of score page numbers on it, but this was certainly not his composition draft, which probably never existed in coherent sequence.

The first performance of *The Black Knight* in Worcester on 18 April 1893 resulted in two major choral commissions and the launch of his national career. In 1890 Worcester had commissioned the *Froissart* overture for the Three Choirs Festival. Six years later they asked for *The Light of Life*, and the North Staffordshire Festival wanted *King Olaf*. In both works Novello demanded cuts, and in both Elgar made use of music he had written previously for other purposes. In the short oratorio, 'O Thou, in heaven's dome' enshrines music originally intended as an Ophelia song from *Hamlet* Act 4 Scene 5. At the start of 'The Death of Olaf' Elgar makes use for the first six lines of his first 'Mill-wheel Song', composed three years before to words by his wife. This was increasingly Elgar's practice as his sketchbooks multiplied so that such late works left incomplete by Elgar as Symphony No. 3 and *The Spanish Lady* were to have been based on ideas that came to him many years previously and originally in a different context.

From his earliest days Elgar was an expert extemporizer, and it is no accident that the *Enigma Variations* of 1899 (perhaps still his finest orchestral work) began in just such an idle fashion after a tough day's violin teaching. The thematic play is so subtle, accomplished and apparently effortless that it seems the work might go on for ever. It is the stranger, therefore, that Elgar often seems straitjacketed by the traditional demands of sonata form and is notably wary of development sections. If possible, he likes to skip development altogether, as for instance in the finale of the Violin Concerto or the slow movement of Symphony No. 2. A preferred alternative is to launch on new material, as with the 'devil of a fugue' in the Introduction and Allegro, and the central sections of *Cockaigne* and *In the South*. Novello marked the arrival of the *Variations*, an incontrovertible masterpiece conducted by the Hans Richter who had initially directed Wagner's *Ring* (even though the Meister felt not a single tempo had been right), with the first printing of an Elgar full score.

Elgar's greatest choral work remains *The Dream of Gerontius* (1900). It is easy enough to assess his treatment of Cardinal Newman's poem, the extensive cuts he needed to make, but also the subtle additions he devised in Part II. Eventual performance in Worcester Cathedral meant that Newman's Catholic vision had to be approximated somehow to the theology of the Anglican Thirty-Nine Articles. Much musical material survives to reveal Elgar's thought processes, and an initial 'PLAN' was made for the end of both parts. But throughout the sketches and drafts are references to sketchbooks that have since disappeared. Such references as '26 I', '48 II' and '34 III' imply that at least three sizeable sketchbooks were in play (the first figure is the page number). Characteristic borrowings and loans occur. The 'Angel of the Agony' music was originally meant for Judas in *The Apostles*, while ideas for 'And now the threshold, as we traverse it' or 'And that a higher gift than grace' were abandoned until the 1912 *Music Makers*. Sketches for the 'Angel of the Agony' included also a trilled gargling duet for the throats of Elgar and his wife.

Elgar's grandest improvisation involved the two oratorios originally intended as part of a trilogy. This method or lack of it in both *The Apostles* and *The Kingdom* involved Elgar in crises of confidence and near-collapse, so that in neither work did he remotely achieve his original intention. As the date for the 1903 Birmingham performance of *The Apostles* loomed, Novello pleaded for a sight of the libretto. Elgar could not oblige for the good reason that it did not exist. It remains a wonder that, with the *Gerontius* achievement behind him, Elgar seems to have had little conception of how many scenes of how many words he could include in either work. His original intention was to conclude the story at Syrian Antioch, where the disciples were first called Christians, conceivably in a single work. In fact the scheme never gets further than Jerusalem, nor is there space for Stephen, Paul, or Simon Magus, to name only three of the characters who should have appeared. Yet equally remarkable is the fact that both works are not only viable but dramatically convincing.

Elgar's librettos are compiled from biblical snippets garnered in concordances. There was bias towards the Old Testament and Apocrypha, if only because the texts were less familiar. His underlying problem was that the more his music possessed him and drove him towards symphonic elaboration, the fewer scenes could be set. So he indulged himself with Mary Magdalene in Part I of *The Apostles* to the extent that Judas's betrayal and suicide were shifted to Part II and a putative Part III had to be postponed to *The Kingdom*. It was a ramshackle procedure, but somehow Elgar's genius was powerful enough to make it work. He needed some authentic Jewish material, satisfactorily supplied by Rabbi F. L. Cohen; the traditional Latin music of Gregorian chant is used also, not only in direct quotation but also as a main atmospheric component. Elgar became increasingly adept at transitions from quasi-modalism to diatonic harmony and back.

Just as Wagner developed increasing motivic flexibility and resource during the writing of *The Ring*, so it was with Elgar. Themes that are comparatively static in *The Apostles* develop a fluidity in the companion work that is musically more adventurous and satisfying. If the orchestral introduction to Part II of *The Apostles* is cobbled together from a string of juxtaposed motifs with no essential connection, the glowing start to *The Kingdom* has a symphonic sweep that not only looks back to the *Gerontius* prelude but on to the gorgeous orchestral palette of the symphonies. A. J. Jaeger, Elgar's 'Nimrod', had supplied Elgar with eight finely bound sketchbooks in November 1901. Material for the oratorios is in all of them except no. 5. Elgar's reference system was the same as for *Gerontius*, and it was to his obvious advantage in making the vocal score to have pages from different books open before him simultaneously. Such references occur also on sections of the libretto, as Elgar's musical conception advanced *pari passu* with that of the text.

'By the Wayside' neatly exemplifies one of Elgar's compositional processes (he adopted much the same manner for the cadenza of the

Violin Concerto). Initially he constructed a passage of continuous music that should cover the whole movement. He then dismembered it so as to insert the Beatitudes between the different sections according to a key scheme he had dotted down. Elgar scored his music at extraordinary speed and with remarkable certainty. In *The Kingdom*, though, there is one passage that caused him such doubt he decided to replace it with different music when the scoring was already complete. It is part of Peter's sermon in Scene 3, at the words 'and your young men shall see visions, and your old men shall dream dreams'. It is obvious why Elgar's mind reverted to *Gerontius* at this point. Indeed he decided to quote the 'Angel's Farewell' as setting to the text. He realized finally that the associations were wrong, self-indulgently wrong, so substituted the passage of quiet radiance we now know.

The requirement for a symphony became ever more insistent. Richter greatly wanted it, and indeed ultimately received the dedication of Symphony No. 1. In fact much of the material for No. 2 was noted earlier, as Elgar acknowledged in a letter to Richter just before the *Apostles* premiere. He described a car journey in which he notionally reported 'Six (6) babies, run over, at one pound (£1) per baby' and claimed all such incidents were 'being worked into the Symphony in E♭'. The summer of 1907 saw the origin of the great motto tune that begins the First Symphony; at about the same time he began a string quartet, of which at least one seminal passage, the bridge between Scherzo and Adagio, was transferred to the Symphony. And again it is clear from the full score that the Finale section, vaguely reminiscent of an equivalent passage in Brahms's Third Symphony, was an afterthought, inserted when scoring was complete. This had structural implications of major import.

With *Falstaff* (1913) there is no sonata straitjacket. Elgar can conjure his very own fat knight as a tale told sometimes in Shakespearian sequence, sometimes not. A significant hint about the work's structure comes in a letter to the Austrian conductor Ferdinand Löwe, written when he was actually scoring the music. He claimed it would play for 'about 20 minutes', which is such a wild underestimate one must assume the 'Dream Interlude' was not part of the original scheme. It existed independently in G minor (now A minor) and receives no separate mention in Elgar's plans. The *Falstaff* idea went back at least to the first page of Jaeger's sketchbook no. 1, where the name appears as heading. Musical hints appear among sketches for *The Apostles* and the *Rabelais* ballet he toyed with after the oratorio. In sketchbook no. 2 Falstaff jostles Judas, Simon Magus and the Lord's Prayer. A sketch for two bassoons labelled 'Bardolph drunk *fatuous sound*' emphasizes the essential situation with the words 'hic! hic hic hic' over leaps to high notes. Alice Stuart-Wortley's copy of the miniature score has in it a scrap of MS paper inscribed 'Falstaff (tragedy)'.

Elgar reacted variously to the tragedy of the First World War. There were such occasional pieces for war victims as *Carillon*, *Polonia* and *Le drapeau belge*. Most ambitious was *The Spirit of England*, a setting of three Binyon poems and again quoting *The Dream of Gerontius*, though this time the demons' music was characterizing the Germans at war. Most moving, though, was the bleakness of *Une voix dans le désert*, with the temporary consolation of its central song. Most significant for Elgar, perhaps, was the escape world of *The Starlight Express*. Using some of his *Wand of Youth* music to back up a massive three-act score, Elgar entered a never-never world of travel among the constellations in search of stardust that clearly enthralled him. He signed off at the end of the work with his inimitable signature dated 'Dec 1915', drawings of five mice and two prowling cats plus, in tiny symbols, 'ae. 15'. It was wishful thinking, but for the moment he felt a nineteenth-century teenager again.

The received wisdom is that Lady Elgar's death in 1920 snuffed Elgar's creative vitality. Far from it, as has notably been shown in Anthony Payne's realization of the sketches for the Third Symphony. What was most surely removed was the sense of purpose and discipline she so resolutely maintained. From the outset she knew her husband must be a great composer, and he complied. Her death meant that not only the Symphony but also the *Spanish Lady* project remained a torso. Both works were an omnium gatherum of material from the past, but not only that. If the Symphony was to start with 'Antichrist' music originally planned for *The Last Judgement*, the most extended section of *The Spanish Lady* developed Simon Magus themes meant for *The Kingdom*. But there was original freshness in the duetting for the operatic young lovers, and the second subject in the Symphony's opening Allegro was devised specially for Vera Hockman, Elgar's latest Egeria. It was cancer, rather, that snuffed Elgar's brief candle.

6

Elgar the Composer

CHRISTOPHER KENT

Elgar shared with Thomas Hardy similar social and economic barriers that denied them 'the polish of a University'.[1] Claire Tomalin's recent study of Hardy[2] has shown that enforced self-tuition was as much a positive advantage to him as it was to be for Elgar. As young boys, both showed precocious creative and expressive potential: the bookish Hardy danced ecstatically to his father's violin-playing, Elgar was found on a river bank trying to write down 'what the reeds were singing' on a piece of paper with five stave lines. As Elgar's biographers have successively noted, his studies of treatises on Figured Bass (L. Mozart), Species Counterpoint (Cherubini), Harmony (Stanier and Catel) and Orchestration (Berlioz) were foremost, through his assimilations from these publications, but were underpinned by playing and studying the masterworks of a diverse cross-section of the European heritage repertoire. Towards the end of his life Elgar expressed to Basil Maine his attitudes and feelings towards composition, although these are not without some contradictions: 'I take no credit for the music I write. While I am composing I become a kind of medium; it is not a conscious process.'[3]

'I can only write when the spirit moves me. I cannot write to order.' Yet he declared a distinction between music that took shape poetically and music that he wrote down mechanically.

I take no credit for the inspiration that people may discover in my music, I cannot tell you how it comes to me. Of course I could write out a piece of music here and now, as you would write a letter, mechanically that is to say. But before the real stuff will come, I must be quiet and apart.[4]

There was nothing unusual about Elgar in this respect as Willam Byrd had written 500 years previously: 'I have learned by experience—a mysterious hidden power... the most appropriate strains occur of their own accord in a strange way.'[5]

In the last of his controversial series of lectures as Peyton Professor of Music at the University of Birmingham, Elgar quoted from a letter of Tchaikovsky:

> Do not believe those who try to persuade you that composition is only a cold exercise of the intellect. The only music capable of moving and touching the depths of a composer's soul is that which flows from the depths of a composer's soul when it is stirred by inspiration.[6]

It is not possible within the scope of this chapter to give a complete perspective of Elgar's self-tuition and stylistic growth.[7] In the mid-1870s he arranged Fugues from J. S. Bach's *Well-Tempered Clavier* for string quartet[8]; in 1883, at the age of 26, he composed a 'Fugue for Violin and Oboe', in the style of Bach. Although it features *en passant* in Ken Russell's film of 1957, it remains unpublished, but with the recent availability of a third manuscript source it is now among the most extensively documented of Elgar's early works.[9]

Ex.1. Fugue for Violin and Oboe, revisions to the conclusion,
6 May 1883.

from the final *stretto* shows his crafting of the sequential structure with further figurative detailing, fastidious attention to expressive details, and idiomatic writing, as shown in the final decision to spread the d-f♯ double stop of the violin in the final bar.

As well as Bach, Schumann and Wagner were composers with whom Elgar was to share a predilection for sequences, as he was later to defend in the *Westminster Gazette*:

> The masters from Bach to Wagner are all deeply indebted to [musical waterwheels]. They were masters not because they scorned to use them, but because with them the waterwheel is a mere adjunct to the house and not a pretext for the building. The whole history of music is strewn with the forgotten reputations of those who thought otherwise.[10]

Through the 1890s, Elgar's style matured rapidly: 'the real stuff' flowed more readily. Our knowledge of one of his most well known works from this period, the *Serenade for Strings* Op. 20,[11] has been widened by another manuscript that has recently come into the public domain, an intended fair copy of the first movement, stemming from *Three Pieces for String Orchestra* (Spring Song, Elegy and Finale) of 1888[12] that were the likely genesis of the *Serenade*. It is an intended ink fair copy to which Elgar made a number of pencil revisions, some subtle, others more substantial.[13] Although untitled, and without tempo indications, it reveals that some subtle rhythmic and expressive changes were made to the opening melody and to the answering motif.

Ex.2a. Serenade for Strings, revision of the first movement opening theme.

Ex.2b. Serenade for Strings, further revisions to the phrasing, rhythm and articulation of the first violin part.

Changes were also made to the scoring, at letter B 1–3 where the viola and violoncello parts were reversed. A melodic alteration before the lyrical third theme is a characteristic example of Elgar avoiding a 'commonplace' ending.[14]

Ex.3. Serenade for Strings, revision to the cadence at the third theme of the first movement.

At the climax of the movement (H 1–7) he optimized the sonorities by dividing the cellos giving the upper part the timbre of the tenor register to reinforce the first violins.

It is unfortunate that the intermediate fair copies of the other two movements are not yet in the public domain. However, considerable insight into the evolution of the *Larghetto* can be obtained from the initial working sketches in the British Library.[15] Originally headed *Andante* and in 4/4 time, the pencil sketch of the freely imitative dialogues of the introduction is complete in all essential harmonic and melodic features, but they lead to a different main theme. It is not difficult to appreciate why Elgar replaced this aspiring elegiac melody, limited in its melodic and harmonic interest, and confined to simple diatonic harmonies (but for a gauche chromatic slither) with the wide-ranging sweeping

Ex.4. Serenade for Strings, second movement, replacement of the main theme.

undulations of its successor. Is this a revision that reflects Elgar's acknowledgement of his wife's inspiration? As he wrote, 'Braut helped a great deal to / make these little tunes signed E.E.'[16] It is indeed surprising that the lyrical spontaneity of this work was not achieved without such alterations.

The manuscript of the piano duet version[17] shows that there was also a major revision to the brief finale (*Allegretto*). It was originally to have concluded in G after only 38 bars.

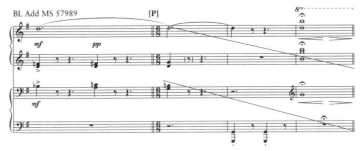

Ex.5. Serenade for Strings, third movement, the original ending.

Elgar subsequently extended the movement by 16 bars (P) with a cyclic return of the two main themes from the first movement interfacing the minor and major modes of E. Indecisions and changes to the conclusions of works abound in Elgar's manuscripts of which the extended coda to the *Variations on an Original Theme* (Enigma) Op. 36 is the most well known. Others include the Second Symphony where there are discarded cadences to three of its movements.

At the end of this decade of rapid stylistic growth came his setting of *The Dream of Gerontius*. Newman's poem, published in 1886, was declined by Dvořák as a text to set for the Birmingham Festival of 1887, but prior to Elgar it was set by the Revd Samuel James Rowton (1844–1930) for soli, eight and twelve part chorus and orchestra. Rowton's score, apparently unpublished, has yet to be found.[18] Though Elgar's setting of *Gerontius* is a work of genius and fervent commitment, not all may agree it to be a work of assured maturity. By reducing the text of Newman's poem from 900 to 435 lines Elgar concentrated and expedited the drama (Part I has 170 lines, of which 33 lines were deleted; Part II has 730 lines reduced to 300). However, the perception and persistence of Jaeger secured the orchestral representation of the apotheosis as the Soul of Gerontius receives a momentary glimpse of Christ in Glory, a challenge from which Elgar had initially recoiled.[19]

Like most of his major works, the sketches for *Gerontius* contain examples of materials being transferred from earlier incomplete projects. His methodical use of sketch books to feed his working drafts was central to his compositional methods. Elgar used three sets of sketch books; the first, known as the Shed Books, were in use until the 1880s, the second set, to which we have only references, would appear to have been in use from the late 1880s until 1901, when they were succeeded by the third set. For reference purposes he gave each volume a roman numeral and used arabic pagination for ease of cross-referencing with his intermediate drafts. Elgar was being less than honest with Jaeger when he wrote to Jaeger on 27 September 1900: 'as usual when a work is out of hand I tear up me sketch books . . . '; yet a year later he was complaining that his sketch books were as rotten as his editor and ordered the third set. It is fortuitous that Elgar retained as much MS material as he did (unlike Brahms and Thomas Hardy), and that these sketch books, with many of their related drafts and fair copies, now sit safely in the British Library.[20]

With *Gerontius* there are well-known thematic connections with a projected symphony in memory of General Gordon,[21] the 'Judas' oratorio[22] and with G. R. Sinclair's Bulldog Dan.[23] The numerous references to Volumes II and III of his second set of sketch books contained in the working sketches for all the choruses, except for the Demons, supports Elgar's remark that by 1892 *Gerontius* had 'been soaking' in his mind for seven years.

It is the music for the soloists that contains the most significant developments and revisions. The first attempt at Gerontius's plea 'Jesu have mercy, Mary pray for me' almost expires onto a bleak monotone and the original setting of the overt phrase 'Firmly, I believe and truly' was set to the limpid 'Prayer' theme. Elgar's revision has rests, which sharpen the focus of the word rhythms and galvanize the compelling urgency of the drama.

Ex.6. *The Dream of Gerontius, word setting revisions in Part I (23⁶ & 41³).*

At the end of Part I, Elgar first considered setting the Priest's words 'Go in the name of God' to the orchestral 'committal' theme (originally intended for the projected symphony in memory of General Gordon), but this was replaced by a steady cyclic progression above a D pedal point.

Ex.7. *The Dream of Gerontius, revision of the Priest's commital in Part I (74⁶).*

Although Part II of Newman's poem was considerably shortened, Elgar made a further cut to the part of the Soul of Gerontius before the first entry of the Angel. Originally, the Soul was to have continued with a third verse:

'I had a dream; yes—someone softly said
 'He's dead' [altered by Elgar to 'he's gone'] and then a sigh
went round the room. And then I surely heard a priestly voice
 Cry 'Subvenite', and they knelt in prayer.'

Plate One: The Dream of Gerontius Part II: a deleted section between figs. 7 & 8. B.L. Add. Ms. 47902 ff.131–133.

There are two reasons for the abandoning of this section: a return to the themes of Part I would have destroyed the tranquil momentum of the music associated with the 'soul's passage'; and a flashback to Gerontius' deathbed scene would have been inconsistent with the Soul's state of disembodiment. The Angel's words, 'It is because that thou didst fear that now thou dost not fear' were revised three times. First, they were set as a simple recitative, and then set above the 'Fear' and 'Prayer' themes ending on an indecisive monotone. It was finalized at a very late stage, with a slip of manuscript paper pasted onto the verso of the flyleaf of a proof copy of the vocal score. After being transposed up a fifth this engendered 'one of the broadest and most convincing phrases in the work'.

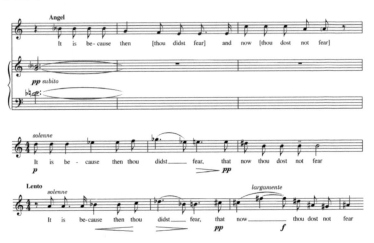

Ex.8. The Dream of Gerontius, Part II, the evolution of the Angel's part fig. 24[1-4].

The initial sketch of the phrase used for the words 'I go before my judge' was originally a threefold sequence of rising minor thirds above a descending whole tone bass. The sketch (with a reference to p. 25 of sketch book II) leads to a theme not used in *Gerontius* but it later found a niche in *The Apostles* for Mary Magdalene's prayer for forgiveness.[24]

It would be inappropriate to confine this discussion of Elgar's setting of *The Dream of Gerontius* to small but significant details. There is also the question of his structural revisions to the work's key relationships. The sketches contain many transpositions, which suggest that keys were interfaced with regard to dramatic contexts within the overall musical structure. With D as the main tonality, in Part I he consistently avoids its dominant, making several transpositions from A to B♭ notably for Gerontius's monologue 'Sanctus fortis' beginning a downward plagal spiral avoiding any keys sharp of the tonic. Thus D and B♭ alternate, apparently symbolizing heavenly and earthly elements, but with the approach of death as the soul is drawn out of the body, the music continues to fall flatwards reaching E♭ minor at the climax of the struggle against death, after which the chorus pulls the music to the most distant key of A♭ minor. Flat keys may be seen to symbolize distance and the spiritual world, yet this preference for 'plagal' relationships was characteristic of Elgar, and the subject of an important letter to Jaeger concerning the First Symphony.[25] It is also notable in *Gerontius* that the keys which feature significantly in Part II are virtually absent from Part I: C and E are associated with the Angel and C also with the Chorus of Angelicals, but there is a return to G minor for the Demons' chorus, and a move to the sharp side of the harmonic spectrum to F♯ major for the words 'the sight of the most fair . . .'.

For a first-hand account of the considerable stress that Elgar experienced when composing 'the real stuff', we have the account of Mrs Richard Powell (Dorabella) in which she describes a visit to Plas Gwyn, Hereford, in late November 1905, when he worked though a day into the small hours at *The Kingdom*. She describes his 'tense expression' and looking 'very pale . . . tired and drawn' during a brief break for dinner and of how he emerged from his locked study soon after 1.30 am: 'the ordeal was now over and one could feel what relief it was. . . . He played through the whole of that evening's work . . . I saw the words: "the sun goeth down: Thou makest darkness, and it is night."'[26] With the experiences of *Gerontius* and *The Apostles*, Elgar had already gained confidence and fluency in working with Wagnerian *leitmotif* structures; the following examples from the sketches for this movement give insights into Elgar's striving for optimum expressive intensity in what must number among the finest movements in High Romantic European oratorio, notwithstanding questions that arise over his commitment to the genre.[27]

Much of the thematic material for *The Kingdom* was drawn from *The Apostles* but the material of the contralto recitative that begins this movement was new: Jaeger described it as a 'grim phrase'.[28] Its earliest source is a five bar pencil sketch[29] with a heavily deleted title which can be deciphered as 'Pomp & C[ircumstance] no 5'.

Ex.9a. The Kingdom: Sc.IV fig. 144⁵, theme originally intended for Pomp and Circumstance March No.5.

Above this are two versions of the motif associated with 'Roman Soldiery' in *The Apostles* each marked 'insert': the first on a C minor dominant, the second on the next system is simple and diatonic; beneath is a third diatonic version in rising 6/3 chords. This 'Grim Phrase' engendered further symphonic growth in the descending sixths of the inner parts of the opening 'Night' theme of the aria.

Ex.9b. The Kingdom: Sc.IV fig. 148¹, transformation of Ex.9a.

Elgar wove into the violin solo of the 'Night' theme metamorphoses of two themes drawn from Pauer's edition of *Traditional Hebrew Melodies*,[30] increasing their expressive plasticity with syncopations and triplets in place of the regular quadruple time patterns. Although he deftly acknowledged his use of some of Pauer's 'broad and appropriate harmonies' of these melodies his departures from them are radical.

Ex.10

Although it is clear that Elgar intended the 'Beatitudes' motif to crown the E♭ *nobilmente* climax of this movement (fig. 159: 'The Gospel of the Kingdom shall be preached in the whole world . . .') it was not finalized without considerable redraftings. The diatonic harmonies of the music suit this visionary ideal, but they are thrown into even sharper relief by the preceding phrase: 'that when his glory shall be revealed . . .' (fig. 156). These features of the theme associated with 'Christ's Glory' where the harmonies are characteristic of the elliptical progressions of Elgar's mature style: chromaticisms where a certain sense of key is temporarily circumvented.

Ex.11. The Kingdom: Sc.IV fig. 156²⁻⁴, harmonic paraphrase.

gives a harmonic paraphrase of this repeated two-bar cell. Its initial sketch is set a tone higher in double note lengths and with a different text. The pencil revisions show the vocal line being drawn out of the orchestral texture, to be enriched with swirling arpeggios.

In the initial sketches for the setting of these words, the first four bars were transposed down to D♭ in order to throw the E♭ climax of the 'Beatitudes' motif (fig. 161) into sharper relief. All of the main elements are present in the earliest draft: *viz.* the 'Gospel', 'Preachers' and 'Beatitudes' motifs as well as the climactic B♭ of the voice part. The sequential repetitions and diminutions which intensify the climax as developed in the subsequent sketches are collated in

Ex.12a.

where it is in E♭ throughout, with an outline accompaniment. The vocal line is secure at the beginning and at the end, but there are uncertainties within the phrase.

Ex.12b.

Ex.12c.

Ex.12. The Kingdom: *Sc IV fig. 159–161, sketches of the growth towards Mary's great vision.*

shows the middle of the phrase expanded into a sequence. This is crossed through in blue pencil and rewritten in diminution above.

Note how Elgar expands the opening of the phrase with a repeat of the rising fourth with the important memo: 'in D♭.' The vocal phrase still ends on the tonic rather than on the exultant third.

Viewed as a whole this context is an example of Elgar's remarks to Sanford Terry that although a climax may be foremost in his mind there is a mass of fluctuating detail, which might fit.[31]

Before considering some aspects of Elgar's Symphony in A♭ Op. 55 it is interesting to observe 'progressive' aspects in two mature miniature pieces: first, the harmonic structure of the F major piano piece *Skizze* (1901) which quotes the 'Sanctus fortis' motif from *Gerontius* above an extended dominant pedal, camouflaged by writhing chromaticisms, and where the tonic resolution is withheld until the coda; second, the Mahlerian progressive tonality of the *Elegy for Strings* Op. 58 (1909) which after beginning with an interface of the major and minor modes of E♭ concludes in C major.

As an essentially orchestral composer of this country it was necessary that his response to the challenge of the German symphonic tradition evolved contiguously with his necessary involvement with the Festival Choral tradition: 'a penalty of my English environment' as he remarked to Delius. Like Vaughan Williams, he emerged slowly as a symphonist; experience and facility grew from the youthful Credo on themes from Beethoven's Symphonies (1873); an incomplete pastiche attempt at the first movement of a symphony based on Mozart's Symphony No. 40 in G minor K.440 (1878); the conversion of the first movement of the Violin Sonata in F K.547 to a Gloria; some complete movements in the Sonata Form mould amongst the wind quintets ('The Farm Yard' and 'Harmony Music No. 2', 1878); two incomplete attempts at environmentally inspired programme overtures; lecture-recitals on each of Beethoven's Violin Sonatas; and culminated in the thematically effusive concert overture *Froissart* Op. 19 (1890). Then came *The Black Knight* Op. 25 (1892), a work he described as a 'Symphony for Chorus and Orchestra' to be followed by the diverse expressiveness and structural assurance of the Organ Sonata in G Op. 28 (1895).

Elgar's ability to remain aloof from the Brahms-versus-Wagner polemic was an advantage of his self-tuition, attending many Wagner performances in England and Germany throughout the 1890s and actively promoting the chamber music of Brahms at concerts in Malvern.[32]

His 'progressivist' tendencies in the mosaics of Wagnerian leitmotifs in *Gerontius* had won the acclamation of Richard Strauss, whose influence is apparent in the concert overture (effectively a tone poem) *In the South* Op. 50 (1904); nevertheless he retained a certain commitment to the abstract symphony. Elgar's assimilations from Schumann's Second Symphony and Brahms's Third Symphony and their parallels in his own work have also been extensively reinvestigated by Michael Gassmann.[33]

These assimilations were the antithesis of the genre as evolved through Beethoven, Brahms or Sibelius, but had more in common with the all-embracing approach of Mahler whose music, although performed in England in the early twentieth century, was not heard by Elgar. Yet any attempt to summarize the ingredients of Elgar's symphonic dialect would be incomplete without acknowledgement of certain elements of Gallic finesse in matters of texture and scoring, in particular, the affection he felt for the style of Saint-Saëns.

The biographical and documentary materials of Elgar's Symphony No.1 in A♭ Op. 55 are extensive.[34] Although he began work in earnest in Rome on 3 December 1907, the motto theme dated from 27 June and the first Trio of the Scherzo from 2 August, and was in common with other projects (Symphony No. 2 in E♭[35] and *Falstaff*[36]), in this instance a String Quartet in D (intended for the Brodsky Quartet) and material intended for the Oratorio trilogy.

The opening motto of the Symphony theme was subject to several alterations after it had replaced an abandoned introduction, which led to the first subject group of the main Allegro.

Ex.13. Symphony No.1 in A♭ I: sketch of the original link from the Introduction to the first theme of the Allegro (fig. 5³).

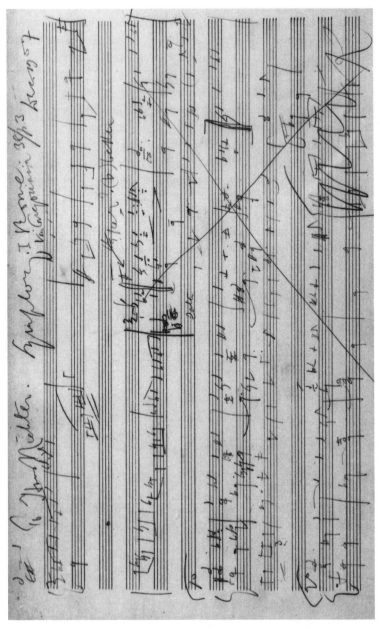

Plate 2: B.L. Add. MS 47907A f.31.

BL Add MS 47907A f.34

Ex.14. Symphony No.I in A♭ I: working sketch from the second subject group showing elaborations and orchestration details.

Much has been made of the apparent A♭-D minor tritonal interface, notwithstanding Elgar's adamant assertion that 'the general key is A♭—the signature of one flat means nothing—it is convenient for the players'. The key of the first subject is A minor, which may be justified as a classical Neapolitan semitonal shift that Elgar recalls at the final cadence of the movement (55 ⁴⁻⁵).

A revision to the first theme of the second subject group contains an example of a revision arising from Elgar's spontaneous orchestral thinking where the countermotifs for the flute and first violins were added in pencil to elaborate the simpler pan-diatonic sixths which are in ink.

Equally significant alongside such important points of detail are Elgar's overview planning sketches for complete movements or extended sections of his music. There are two examples of these for the First Symphony: one covers the metamorphosis of the scurrying perpetuum mobile of the Scherzo to the serenity of the *Adagio*,[37] the other is a musico-literary précis of the *Adagio* itself.

BL Add MS 47907A f.98

Ex.15. Symphony in A♭ III: Elgar's plan for the Adagio.

The working sketches for this movement contain an important example of Elgar's vigilant self-criticism in an alteration to the first violin melody of the second theme.[38] The coda of the *Adagio* predated work on the Symphony, although bound with the working sketches it first appears in C major on a folio possibly removed from a series of sketches for *The Kingdom* dated 21 August 1904.[39] The continuation of 1908 is shown by a change in the shade of the pencil from the triplet motif at the end of the second system.

There are also two abandoned sketches of an Introduction to the Finale.[40] It needs little imagination to understand why they were not used: a gauche cymbal crash followed by strident chords and exuberant figurations was a less-than-subtle sequel to the Shakespearean quotation, 'The rest is silence', at which even the agnostic Jaeger felt 'brought near to Heaven'. In Elgar's ghostly subdued *Adagio*, the revision reintroduces the motto theme fragment of the second theme of the ensuing Allegro. There is evidence that this also

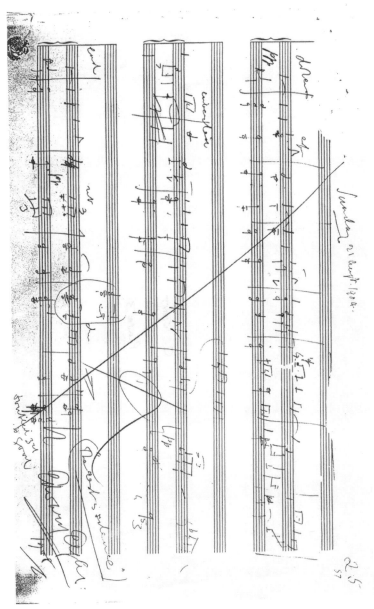

Plate 3: Symphony in A♭, Coda of the Adagio, sketch of 1904
continued in 1908. B.L. Add MS. 47907A f.57

*Ex.16. Symphony in A♭ IV: the opening of the original intro-
duction to the finale, the second sketch (f.129) features a cymbal
crash [x].*

had a previous incarnation in the sketches of the Oratorio Trilogy
The Kingdom where it appears as a fivefold sequence in rising
thirds.[41]

In the Symphony after some 'boisterous antiphony' its cantabile transformation (fig. 114–116), an eleventh hour insertion made after most of the movement had already been scored.[42] But Elgar's mature confidence in orchestration and scoring is amply evident at the final apotheosis of the motto theme, where the short score diminishes to scant outlines with the remark before ether final cadence: 'fill this up'.[43]

Plate 4: Symphony in A♭: short score outline of conclusion.
(B.L. Add. MS. 47907A f.146).

In conclusion Elgar may have agreed with Tippett that:

Part of the poet's or painter's or the musician's job is just that of renewing our sense of the comely and the beautiful. If in the music I write, I can create a world of sound wherein some, at least, of my generation can find refreshment for the inner life, then I am doing my work properly. It is a great responsibility to try to transfigure the everyday by a touch of the everlasting, born that as always has been, and will be again of our desire.[44]

It is certain that Elgar succeeded in refreshing the inner lives of many of his contemporaries, and there is little doubt that the beauty and exquisite sensitivity of his music will continue to enrich the lives of future generations as well as our own.

Notes

1 E. W. Elgar (ed. P. M. Young), *A Future for English Music and Other Lectures* (London: Dennis Dobson, 1968), pp. 47–523.

2 C. Tomalin, *Thomas Hardy: The Time-torn Man* (London: Viking, 2006), p. 68.

3 B. Maine, *Elgar: His Life and Works* (London: Bell, 1933), Vol. II p. 208.

4 Ibid. p. 77.

5 Preface to *Gradualia* I (1607).

6 Elgar, *A Future for English Music*, p. 219.

7 The present writer is currently writing an extended study of Elgar's stylistic evolution in which this will be considered further.

8 C. Kent, 'Elgar and J. S. Bach: A Wider Perspective', *Irish Musical Studies 5* (1995) 179–190.

9 Sotheby's Music Sale, 1 December 2005, lot 56.

10 E. Elgar, 'Musical Waterwheels', *The Westminster Gazette* 13 May 1915.

11 Breitkopf and Haertel, 1893.

12 R. Burley and F. C. Carruthers, *Edward Elgar: The Record of a Friendship* (London: Barrie and Jenkins, 1972), p. 31.

13 Elgar Birthplace Museum, Broadheath, Worcester, MS ref 137.

14 Letter to August Jaeger, 26 March 1906, in E. Elgar (ed. P. M. Young), *Letters to Nimrod* (London: Dobson, 1965), pp. 256–8.

15 B.L. Add. Ms. 47900a f.22.

16 B.L. Add. MS. 57989, piano duet arrangement, dated May 13 1892.

17 Ibid f.12.

18 J. D. Brown and S. S. Stratton, *British Musical Biography*, Birmingham, (publisher), 1897, p. 357.

19 J. N. Moore (ed.), *Elgar and His Publishers: Letters of a Creative Life* (2 Vols, Oxford: Clarendon Press, 1987), Vol. I, pp. 191–209.

20 B.L. Add. MSS. 63146–63150 & 63153–63162. Elgar's MSS as a whole contain a considerable residue of floating materials some of which relate to unpublished or incomplete scores (e.g. *Callicles*, *The Last Judgement*, *King Arthur*, *Beau Brummel*, Piano Concerto, Symphony No. 3, etc.), which have been compared to a 'ticking time bomb' (*q.v.* B. Adams, 'Elgar's Later Oratorios' in D. M. Grimley and J. Rushton (eds), *The Cambridge Companion to Elgar* (Cambridge: Cambridge University Press, 2004), p. 82). These may yet continue to be sources of inspiration to the courageous.

21 Moore, *Letters of a Creative Life*, Vol. I, pp. 92–4, 96, 108.

22 Ibid. p. 151.

23 P. M. Young, *Elgar OM, A Study of a Musician* (London: Collins, 1955), p. 399.

24 Grimley and Rushton, *The Cambridge Companion to Elgar*, p. 43.

25 Moore, *Letters of a Creative Life*, Vol. II, p. 710.

26 Mrs R. Powell, *Edward Elgar: Memories of a Variation* (4th revised edn, Aldershot: Scholars Press, 1994), pp. 89–93.

27 B. Adams, 'Elgar's Later Oratorios', pp. 81–105

28 A. J. Jaeger, *The Kingdom, Analysis and Book of Words*, (London) Novello, 1906, p. 39.

29 B.L. Add. 63154 f.*12v.*

30 E. Pauer (ed.), *Traditional Hebrew Melodies*, Augener, Ed. No 8295, n.d.; *Al Elleh* 'Hymn of Weeping' 29, and *Hamabdil* 'Hymn of Parting' 8.

31 Sketches in the Library of The Athenaeum.

32 E. Elgar, 'Brahms's Chamber Music' *The Malvern Gazette*, 21 December 1886 & 29 January 1887.

33 Michael Gassmann *Edward Elgar und die Deutsche Symphonische Tradition*, (Studien und Materialien zur Muiskwissenschaft bd. 27), Olm, Hildesheim, 2002, p. 197.

34 B.L. Add. Ms. 47907A 110ff. of working sketches. Related materials in Sketch Books B.L. Adds. MSS 63155, 63160, 63162, and a fragment at The Elgar Birthplace Museum, ref. 619. B.L. Add. MS 58024. Full score, The Elgar Birthplace ref. 1453, proofs.

35 C. Kent, 'A View of Elgar's Methods of Composition through the Sketches of the Symphony No.2 in E♭ Op.63', *Proceedings of the Royal Musical Association*, ciii (1976–77); pp. 41–60.

36 C. Kent, '*Falstaff*: Elgar's Symphonic Study' in R. Monk (ed.), *Edward Elgar: Music and Literature* (Aldershot: Scholars Press, 1993), pp. 83–107.

37 E. W. Atkins, *The Elgar-Atkins Friendship* (Newton Abbot: David and Charles, 1984), p. 194.

38 Grimley and Rushton, *The Cambridge Companion to Elgar*, p. 46.

39 B.L. Add. Ms. 47904A f.87 is paginated 25 & 26 in Elgar's hand; this is missing from B.L. Add. MS 63155 (Sketch Book III).

40 B.L. Add. MS. 47907A ff. 91*v.* & 129.

41 B.L. Add. MS. 47907A f.114*v.* is paginated 55 in Elgar's hand which is a missing leaf from B.L. Add. MS 63159 (Sketch Book VII).

42 R. Anderson, *Elgar in Manuscript*, London, The British Library, 1990, pp. 101–2.

43 B.L. Add. MS. 47907A f.122.

44 M. Tippett, *Moving into Aquarius*, London, Routledge & Kegan Paul, 1959, p. 12.

7

Elgar the Progressive

HANS KELLER

The title of this chapter is, of course, a variation on Schoenberg's 'Brahms the Progressive'. Schopenhauer used to be very hard on people who didn't invent their own brand-new titles, but then Schopenhauer used to be very hard on everybody except Plato, Shakespeare, Kant, Goethe, poodles and Schopenhauer. For myself, I think that variation does or does not mean something *qua* variation, and my title does.

Schoenberg was out to show that 'Brahms, the classicist, the academician, was a great innovator in the realm of the musical language', that, in fact, he was 'a great progressive'. Now, Elgar was not an academician, and the question of what kind of an '-icist' you consider him would seem to depend on which of the astonishing diversity of standpoints manifest in the literature on his music you want to adopt. But we are all agreed that, among other things, he was a Brahmsian and a Wagnerian—the latter, to be sure, an aspect which has been vastly exaggerated outside the oratorios.

Anyhow, nobody has yet credited him with much creative futurity; even Donald Mitchell, in an essay of exceptional originality, points out that 'the remoteness, for our century, of Elgar's idiom, does stress his singular isolation as a composer', and assumes as self-evident 'that he had no hand in forming the musical language of our own day'. It is true that he goes on to qualify, reminding us that both Elgar's sheer competence and his cosmopolitanism foreshadow the future, but he never doubts for a moment that Elgar's style was of no significance for the further development of composition.

My own submission, with which I want to close the Elgar Year by way of complimentary realism, is the opposite. *Mutatis mutandis*, I find that Elgar's musical language is what Schoenberg says Brahms's is, rather than what Mitchell says Elgar's is. Specifically, Elgar's innovations are quite different from Brahms's, of course, but they are there, demonstrably so; nor do I propose to point, for the hundredth time, to the muted *pizzicato tremolo* in the fiddle concerto's *cadenza accompagnata*; I do mean genuine innovations of language. In fact, it will be seen that strictly speaking Schoenberg's statement is truer of Elgar than of Brahms, because where Schoenberg is largely concerned with the rhythmic structure and motivic or thematic organization, aspects which are not normally included in the concept of 'musical language', Elgar's innovations fall neatly into this category and could not be described in any other way.

The most relevant starting-point for our investigation is the question of Elgar's Englishness. It is in the face of this question, too, that the diversity of commentators' views reaches extremes. Everett Helm recalled

> ... a widely held opinion that Elgar is a very 'English' composer. I'm inclined to agree ... There does appear to be a certain quality in his music that appeals to many of his countrymen and escapes, or even rebuffs, a 'foreigner'.
>
> This quality can scarcely be defined in words, and it has nothing whatever to do with 'folksiness'. Elgar had very little use for folk song as an ingredient of concert music, and it would seem most unlikely that he ever strove consciously to 'sound English' ...
>
> By this exclusive 'English' quality I do mean Elgar's *Pomp and Circumstance* vein which is a surface phenomenon and can be discounted, or ignored, as such ...

This may be said to correspond to the traditional viewpoint. Donald Mitchell's counterblast, actually published a month earlier, represents an anti-traditionalist attitude:

> Elgar's convention was thoroughly post-Wagnerian in character,

English, in any stylistic sense, not at all . . . It has, I must confess, always astonished me that Elgar has been so strenuously claimed as a representative English figure.

And again:

It is my view that to find Elgar today specifically English in flavour is to expose oneself as a victim of a type of collective hallucination, an achievement, incidentally, that has had its consequences abroad.

Mitchell is not slow to substantiate his novel assertion and to crystallize its aesthetic implications:

Elgar [as opposed to Mahler and Stauss] was encumbered by no tradition. He could handle his more conventional convention with all the enthusiasm of an early starter; the convention simply had not aged for him as it had for his contemporaries in Europe. The oddity of his English situation spared him the necessity of composing, as it were, with history at his elbow. Free of the burden of a tradition, he was able, as an outsider—he owes England, this much, at least—to employ a convention that had grown old elsewhere . . . at an earlier stage in its development; and the power and, indeed, originality of his musical personality changed his—from history's point of view—conventionalities with a conviction and spontaneity that will ride out any fluctuations in fashion.

In a big lawsuit before a *cadi*, the plaintiff had just finished his case. The *cadi* meditated, then said, 'You're right, but let's hear the defendant now.' The defendant, angered into brilliance by the *cadi*'s apparent prejudgement, disproved the plaintiff's case with great skill. The *cadi* meditated and then said 'You're right too.' At this, a law student in the public gallery couldn't hold himself any longer and shouted, 'But *cadi*, they can't both be right at the same time!' The *cadi* meditated, then said, 'You're right too.'

I accept the ruling of the *cadi*. Both Mitchell and Helm are right, and if the reader thinks they can't both be right at the same time, he's right too, because there's nothing wrong with either view.

In media res. As my single example, whose analysis is intended to offer the reader the tools for the analysis of any instance of Elgar's stylistic innovations, I am choosing the first subject of the *Introduction and Allegro* for strings.

The reason for my choice is that it is one of the simplest examples I have been able to find of what, in my submission, is the innovatory aspect of Elgar's idiom, and that, at the same time, it evinces all the essential characteristics that distinguish the countless other examples which fairly prolonged attention to this underestimated master's music has elicited.

Within two seconds, i.e. as soon as we hear *p1* in Ex. 1, part of Helm's suggestion—that fact of Elgar's Englishness—is strikingly confirmed, whereas another part—the proposition that 'it has nothing whatever to do with folksiness'—evaporates into thin air. In fact, the English quality of this thought is nowise 'elusive' analytically: it can very well 'be defined in words'. What is presented here is a firmly established tonal penta-scale, which dominates both the foreground and the background of the melodic line. The notes of *p1*, that is to say, are pentatonic throughout, while at the same time the melodic background—Ex. 2's *p0*—consists of the straight, ascending pentatonic scale itself.

Elgar, the folk-song-hater, harboured a strong folkish tendency without knowing it. The reason why it 'eluded' him and Helm and indeed everybody else is that he had assimilated it so thoroughly, unconsciously, elementally, in his Continental, diatonic idiom (so strongly stressed by Mitchell) that it does not in any way form a contrast to this diatonicism itself: it is a case of utter absorption rather than of mere combination.

The nature of this merging process becomes immediately clear when we pursue the further course of Ex. 1: without any attempt at antithesis, contrast, or rhythmic variation, indeed without any friction whatsoever, the diatonic degrees (*d*) ensue in the continuation and, climax over, recede again, leaving the tonal penta-scale (*p2*) once more alone in the field.

Widening common technical usage without any risk of ambiguity, I propose to call this stylistic characteristic Elgar's modal tendency, including as it does, as occasion arises, the pentatonic scale, the modes proper, or both. As a matter of aesthetic or creative principle, these distinctions are of no importance in the present context.

I don't think it is difficult to see why Helm, an American in Europe, senses this modal tendency even though he cannot define it, whereas Mitchell, an Englishman, flatly denies Elgar's Englishness, drawing attention, very penetratingly so, to the overpowering Continental roots of Elgar's stylistic make-up. Mitchell is quite right when he says that 'Elgar was encumbered by no tradition', but the proposition is only true if it confines itself to what we might call a national art tradition. For below it, there are the early folkloristic influences to which Mitchell, like Elgar, was inevitably subjected, and which therefore, for both of them, are natural to the point of utter unobtrusiveness. The Central-European musical mind, on the other hand, reacts strongly to, and often against, folk scales, modal flavours, however concealed: compare Helm's sensitive remark about the 'certain quality' in Elgar's music 'that appeals to many of his countrymen' while intending to 'rebuss a "foreignger"'. It is probably because I myself am of Continental origin and naturalized in this country, not only legally but also, to some considerable extent, musically, that I am spontaneously able to trace and isolate Elgar's modal tendency despite its usually heavy concealment.

Contrary to the views that are now the prevailing fashion among those who (for very strong if personal reasons) prefer 'advanced' playing-about to creating, real innovations, which mean something as a mainspring of future creative thought, are never experimental.

They always spring from a very deep expressive need; in psycho-logical terms, they thus are always promoted by infantile energies. In other words, it is a paradoxical fact that all genuine revolutions are conservative, in that they conserve an infantile set of dynamic expressions, 'memory traces' in psychoanalytical parlance, and utilize them towards the expression of something altogether new. You cannot be grown-up artistically without the courage to submit to the ferocious power of your infantile unconscious, though the *act* of submission must of course be active, controlled by your insight, your ability to express the generally valid part of yourself in the clearest possible form, and your evolved methods of dealing with this task. Elgar's unconscious, infantile folklorism forced his sophisticated Continental style into an act of submission by natu-ralization: 'I am submitting to you by taking you into my home because there I can control you', says Elgar's Continental language to the folk scales. The act is of course itself unconscious; in fact, Elgar's conscious aversion to folk-song promotes the control of the infantile material. At the same time, Freud's 'return of the repressed' makes itself felt in the work under consideration, whose second subject was consciously inspired by a group of Welsh singers!

This diatonic naturalization of a primitive modal tendency is something so entirely new that Elgar has not yet been fully understood; so new, too, that the most far-reaching, if as yet unrecognized consequences have ensued.

Newness first, lack of understanding second, futurity third:

1) It is true, of course that nineteenth-century music, including even the anti-modal Austro-German tradition, shows modal influ-ences, but the modes are always treated and—in good pieces —functionalized as foreign bodies within the diatonic context; they are never naturalized by it. Brahms himself, Elgar's overpowering father figure, is an excellent example. I am thinking not only of such obvious instances as what I believe to be the well-known combina-tion of Phrygian and Mixolydian in the slow movement theme of the E-minor Symphony, but also of the less stressedly 'advertised' un-diatonicisms, such as the pentatonic opening of the Violin Concerto: even here, that is to say, Brahms uses modality (in the wider sense) as an insurance against sentimentality—his lifelong

fear. Such a procedure is of course only possible in a basically anti-modal musical culture. The kind of thing Brahms was afraid of in this particular instance can be imagined in view of the canonic theme from the César Franck Violin Sonata, where the descent from the mediant over the submediant to the dominant does now eschew the leading note. I do not wish to create the impression that I consider the Franck theme sentimental; on the contrary, I think that the so-felt sentimentality Brahms was afraid of, and which he successfully inhibited, wouldn't have been sentimentality either if he had let it out. In my opinion, he was fighting an internal windmill. In any case, not even he, one of the most scrupulously consistent of masters, ever succeeded in naturalizing the modes into the diatonic idiom, although, as functional foreign bodies, as antitheses, they certainly played a more natural role in his music than his gipsy-isms which, slow movement from the Clarinet Quintet apart, remained as artificial as did the pentatonicism of Dvořák—who, to be sure, in his turn made a virtue of artificiality in such pieces as the simple Violin Sonatina (as distinct from the 'American' Quartet or the 'New World' Symphony).

Elgar's innovations in the field, then, remain something absolutely unprecedented.

2) Reverting to Helm, we find a typical symptom of my conviction that this side of Elgar's is in fact too new to render his music as yet fully comprehensible:

> If Elgar wrote too many notes vertically, producing a thick texture, he also exercised too little restraint on the horizontal plane. There are many passages in which the instruments rush about in semiquavers, demisemiquavers and hemidemisemiquavers with no apparent purpose. One has the impression of motion for motion's sake—of extraordinary hustling and bustling that leads nowhere. This sort of aimless activity mars (for me at least) the *Introduction and Allegro* for strings. The musical motivation in the opening flourish is not clear, nor is it in such passages as the one between figures 10 and 15 of the score. What is accomplished by these and similar passages that recur in other compositions? What expressive purpose do they serve?

If, consequent upon our analysis, Mr Helm will have another look at the score, he will no doubt give his own positive answer to the rhetorical questions. The opening flourish he questions discloses a wonderful anticipatory naturalization of the ensuing tonal penta-scale, and as soon as one has understood this stylistic function, the correlative formal function with its underlying elementally expressive motive power becomes clear in one stroke. Most significantly, too, Helm's next criticism sets in at the precise point (figure 10) where Elgar's modal tendency surges further afield, again forcing the diatonic idiom to naturalize it without friction. As I have intimated before, it is not necessary for me to analyse another passage and insult the reader's own analytic powers: by now you will notice yourself how Elgar is here embarking upon a naturalization of the transposed Phrygian mode.

3) As for the influence on the future, it will, I feel sure, suffice if I mention the most shining examples of later and even better, free-er naturalizations of modality, i.e. the many masterpieces of Benjamin Britten's in which this process can be heard to continue where Elgar left off. It is very likely that Britten loathes Elgar as much as Elgar loathed folk-songs, and that this loathing represents a similar psychological help towards controlling his powerful infantile material which, most probably, includes early impressions of Elgar's music.

'It seems', says Schoenberg at the end of his essay, ' . . . that some progress has already been made . . . in the direction toward an unrestricted musical language which was inaugurated by Brahms the Progressive.' I don't think I need labour the parallel.

8

Elgar's Church Music

ADRIAN PARTINGTON

The ghost of Elgar was everywhere in Worcester Cathedral when I was a small boy. I saw him in the north nave aisle in his favourite position for cathedral concerts, sitting listening to Evensong in the darkened nave, striding around College Yard, cigarette in mouth, intent on some important business. More tangibly, I heard him, when we sang my favourite anthem at Evensong, 'The Spirit of the Lord', or when I attended Festival concerts, most obviously *The Dream of Gerontius* in 1969. There were still many people around the Cathedral who had known Elgar well. I enjoyed conversations with Edgar Day (Assistant Organist at Worcester 1909–1963), who had played in so many concerts which Elgar had conducted, or with Derrick Bollen, who had been a Voluntary Choir-boy in the 1920s and had run weekly errands to Elgar for the then Cathedral Organist, Sir Ivor Atkins, or, indeed, with Sir Ivor's son, Wulstan, who was a frequent visitor to Worcester during my years as a chorister and the author of a fascinating book, *The Elgar-Atkins Friendship*. The place seemed to be soaked in Elgar's influence, and still seems so.

It wasn't only the stones of Worcester and its elder citizens that bore witness to Elgar's continued presence. The Cathedral Organist when I was a boy was the consummate musician and Elgar devotee, Christopher Robinson. It was his idea, together with Brian Culverhouse, a producer for EMI, to record in 1969 an LP of the church music of Elgar. This recording has retained its place in the affections of those who love Elgar's music, and is still, as I write, available for purchase. I played a small part in that recording and remember the sessions clearly, although nearly forty years have passed: the choir stood on the chancel steps, facing the great west window; and I recall being transported by the aesthetic experience of performing this music, sometimes tender, sometimes stirring, as the evening sun slipped lower behind that great blue window, occasionally shooting red at us (for example through the curious scarlet lobster in one of the lights!).

We had not known the music before preparation for the recording had begun earlier in that term, with the single exception of *Ave verum*, which we had sung in the Choir School Chapel Choir. I had felt, aged 8 or 9, that *Ave verum* was rather a dull little piece, and very weak and lacking in pathos beside Mozart's setting of the same text. So I was unprepared for the excitement of the bigger pieces in the recording, particularly the *Te Deum*, which thrilled me.

Listeners to gramophone recordings must have had a similar experience to mine, since it is my impression that few people in the 1960s knew the majority of Elgar's church music; indeed few knew more than the obvious big pieces of the rest of his compositional output. Possibly this is why I have read the word 'groundbreaking' connected with this 1969 recording. There have been many Elgar church music discs made since (including one more from Worcester in the 1980s, for which I was the organist), and probably many more will be made for each Elgar anniversary that comes along. But the first will remain just that, and irreplaceable.

The pieces chosen for that LP were representative of Elgar's church composition; but it was not, nor could it be, given the time restrictions on an LP, a comprehensive collection. However, it did include examples of both of the principal classifications of this music, i.e. firstly works written whilst Elgar was employed as a church musician and, second, the later works written for specific commissions.

Elgar was a church musician from 1872 to 1889, so it is fair to assume that he was immersed in the history, the liturgy and of course the music of the Church. But we are not talking here about the Church of England, although that played a big part in Elgar's life, too, but about the Roman Catholic Church. Elgar was associated with St George's Church, Sansome Place, Worcester, the principal Catholic church in Worcester. This church was dedicated in 1830, a year after the Catholic Emancipation Act. From its opening, the authorities at St George's sought to encourage a strong musical tradition. Elaborate choral and instrumental music was frequently performed at the principal services, with the indigenous choristers and instrumentalists often supplemented by visiting freelance professionals, both vocal and instrumental. It was into this seemingly strong musical tradition that Elgar's father, William, arrived as organist in 1846.

In his *Notes on Catholic Worcester*, the printer and later choirmaster of St George's, Hubert Leicester, wrote the following:

> Prior to W. H. Elgar's appointment, the choir had already gained a distinguished reputation . . . the character of the music and its rendering attracted many singers, both Catholic and Protestant to join the choir, which [was] justly claimed to be one of the most . . . talented in the West of England.

It is not certain that Elgar Senior was ideally suited for this organist's post. He had arrived in Worcester in 1841 to pursue a career as a piano-tuner, teacher, organist and violinist, and he later co-managed a music shop near the cathedral; but, according to his son Edward, 'he never did a stroke of work in his life'! This seems unfortunate, in view of the duties he was expected to perform at St George's: choosing all the music, rehearsing all the musicians, playing the organ, and also composing. William Elgar confessed, however, that the priest 'expects me to do these things—but I don't . . . feel inspired, my mind wanders too much . . .' Additionally, William refused to take any interest in the religious side of his work. He was not a Roman Catholic, and 'cordially detested the whole business'. He ranted about 'the absurd superstition and playhouse mummery of the Papist'.

Edward was, thanks to his mother, Anne, raised as a Roman Catholic, a fact that contributed to his feeling that he was an 'outsider' from respectable society for the rest of his life. However, this mattered to him little when he was a teenager, anxious to learn all he could about his chosen craft of music. 'Chosen', because he had been sent to work at the age of fifteen in a solicitor's office, but after an increasingly unhappy year had obtained his parents' consent to pursue a musical career via as many avenues as possible. He wasted no time, studying the violin, the organ and as much music as he could find both in his father's music shop and St George's church.

It is from these years as a church music apprentice that Edward's earliest liturgical compositions survive. Elgar the composer, of course, was self-taught. He had a hunger to absorb and understand music which must have been intense, to say the least. He began to arrange and re-order instrumental works by, for example, Mozart and Beethoven as Mass movements; there exists, for example, a Credo crafted out of themes from the symphonies of Beethoven, and a Gloria arranged from a violin sonata of Mozart.

In the autumn of 1876 he wrote his earliest surviving original works for the choir of St George's church; a *Salve Regina* and a *Tantum ergo*. The latter, in particular, is a satisfying miniature. An opening, homophonic quartet, with a distinctive falling sixth in the soprano part, is reprised and then developed by the full chorus, with snatches of counterpoint and some rather 'Victorian' harmony. The middle section begins as a ghostly soprano duet in the subdominant minor, but after a brief sequence, a return to the tonic is prepared and the recapitulation is duly delivered. In this piece there are echoes of much of the music that Elgar was known to have been studying at that time: Rossini, Meyerbeer and Weber, not to mention Handel.

But the most potent influence on Elgar's style at this time is the music which Elgar heard, and borrowed, from the great Anglican cathedral at the other end of the High Street. Elgar often related in later life how he used to attend as many services and rehearsals of the Cathedral Choir as possible in these years. The then Cathedral Organist, Dr William Done, seems to have taken a kindly interest in Elgar, who must have come to know very well the music of Crotch, Battishill, Goss, *et al.*; and, especially, that of S. S. Wesley.

Elgar, in fact, encountered S. S. Wesley's music making first hand during these years. The following is taken from Sir Ivor Atkins's address to the Royal College of Organists in July 1935:

Elgar heard him at Worcester in 1875, and often spoke to me of the thrilling effect Wesley's playing had upon him. The occasion was the outgoing voluntary at a Three Choirs Festival Evensong. Wesley began with a long extemporization, designed to lead up to Bach's Choral Prelude 'Wir glauben all an einen Gott' (the Giant Fugue), breaking off the extemporization in an arresting way before entering upon the Prelude. The effect upon Elgar was so great that in after years when he returned to live in Worcester and would constantly slip into the old cathedral which had so many memories for him and which he greatly loved, he almost invariably asked me to play him something, and we always had to end with the 'Giant'. But I do not know if I was ever able to recapture the impression left upon him by Wesley.

Elgar succeeded as organist in 1886; but it seems that the musical establishment at St George's was not what it once was. In fact Elgar's father was not happy about the young man taking on the post. 'The old man does not take kindly to the organ biz; but I hope 'twill be all right before I commence my "labours",' wrote Elgar to his friend Dr Buck in October 1885; but he continued early the next year to say that things were far from alright: 'I am a fully fledged organist now and HATE it. I expect another three months will end it; the choir is awful and no good to be done with them.'

The choirmaster at St George's was Elgar's friend Hubert Leicester, already quoted above. He and Edward produced a set of regulations in an attempt to stop the rot, together with this peremptory note:

In order to put the choir on a satisfactory footing, and to ensure regular and punctual attendance at the Services and rehearsals, we find it necessary to request you to sign the enclosed Conditions of Membership . . . if you wish to remain a member.

One of the regulations was this autocratic sentence:

The members to conform in all musical matters to the instruction of the Organist, whose authority on all questions of Music shall be supreme.

On 9 October 1888, the Archbishop of Birmingham visited St George's Church. For the ceremony, Elgar produced a new anthem, *Ecce sacerdos magnus*. This is a short but noble work, whose main theme undoubtedly resembles the Benedictus theme from Haydn's matchless *Harmoniemesse*, but this is in no way a derivative composition. It has several characteristic Elgarian touches: the ostinato crotchet bass line (cf. the First Symphony, Introduction), the broad sweep of the melody, particularly at the phrase 'in diebus suis placuit' towards the end (cf. the phrase for 'even as many as the Lord' in Part 3 of *The Kingdom*), and the very detailed dynamics, for example the signs sf and rf are used in close proximity—can choirs really distinguish between these? The whole piece is assured, dignified and clearly written by a composer on the verge of defining his own style. The advance in style and technique on the *Tantum ergo* is striking.

There are two further groups of short works which need to be mentioned from Elgar's time at St George's apart from the other small and immature fragments. The first group consists of three settings of the communion motet *O salutaris hostia*, written, it seems, at different stages of Elgar's time at St George's. The first is a charming a cappella, strophic setting, which possibly dates from 1872. It is characterized by a wide-ranging melody, and the inevitable sub-Mendelssohnian harmony. The second setting was not published until 1898 (in Tozer's *Complete Benediction Manual*), but must have been written much earlier, judging by its student-like characteristics—probably in the late 1870s. It is in the style of a slow minuet, which seems somewhat inappropriate to the text, as do the jaunty dotted rhythms and acciaccaturas which abound. The organ part is only occasionally independent from the choir, but when it is, it is awkward to play, with its chains of parallel sixths. The third is a much more successful aesthetic experience. It was published in 1888 in Cary's *Modern Church Music*, but was written in 1880. It is sensitive and devout, and really sounds 'Elgarian': for example, the modulations to the mediant and submediant, the soprano melody and associated harmony in the second phrase—the second inversion chord under the word 'fer' is affecting and typical—and most importantly, the quasi sequence beginning at the words 'Bella premunt', with its 'animato' feel, its incidental dissonances and its quickly subsiding climax; all these things can be found in the works of Elgar's maturity.

It has to be said that none of the works so far discussed featured on the LP which I mentioned at the start. The *Three Aves* Op. 2, however, did. These are famous pieces now, and very beautiful. *Ave verum* started life as a setting of *Pie Jesu* (itself a re-working of an earlier Kyrie), which was written for the funeral of one William Allen in 1887. Allen had been a member of the St George's congregation, and Elgar's employer in the solicitor's office where he worked for a year. In 1902, Elgar, by now a national figure, sought out his *Pie Jesu* and re-worked it as an *Ave verum*. The impetus for Elgar to do this was the knowledge that the directors of the great publishing house of Novello were considering offering him a blanket contract to publish everything that he wrote. Elgar, as usual, was concerned about money and decided to send Novello some simple trifles which he hoped might make the company money, which in turn might persuade them to publish the big and serious works he had it in mind to write. He wrote to his great friend and supporter at Novello, A. J. Jaeger, in January a now famous and rather miserable letter, which includes this:

> . . . my things are successful among musicians, but the public don't buy them . . . my music does not arrange well for the piano, and consequently is of no commercial value. If I had a free mind I shd. like to write my chamber music, and symphony etc., etc., on all of which forms of art Providence has laid the curse of poverty . . . But Providence, as I've often told you, is against all art . . .

Ave verum is in a concise, tuneful style, and makes use of the statement and reprise technique which pervades so much Catholic church music, for example the litany (Elgar wrote four litany settings, as well as the brief quasi-litany in *Gerontius*). It is light and cheerful, and makes little attempt to illustrate the poignancy of the text. The four-bar coda still seems to me a sentimental miscalculation; but despite this, the piece, as we have already learned, kept its place in the repertory until the 1960s, when most of its colleagues had vanished.

In June 1907, Elgar reached his fiftieth birthday. It was his habit to view each temporal milestone as an opportunity to look back over his life. Some days before the anniversary, he looked out some fragments from his past—symbols of 'time vanished never to return' (J. N. Moore). These fragments he re-worked as two more motets, *Ave Maria* and *Ave maris stella*. He sent them to Novellos with a note which read, 'They are tender little plants so treat them kindly whatever is their fate.'

Novello published the *Three Aves* as Elgar's Op. 2. *Ave Maria* is a strong, passionate miniature, with a surging climax and huge variety. The intense unison, 'Ora pro nobis', is particularly effective; the usual plethora of performance directions are judicious and necessary. *Ave maris stella* returns to the mood and key (G major) of *Ave verum*. It is hymn-like in character and makes use of two soprano soloists, who present the majority of the melodic material. There are some good touches (e.g. the whispered ATB accompaniment refrain *Ave maris stella*), but this simple piece does not reach the emotional heights of its predecessor.

The Op. 2 set of motets are the last pieces which date from the years when Elgar was in church employment. He ceased to be associated with St George's a week before his marriage to Caroline Alice Roberts in May 1889. A note in his diary suggests a feeling of relief that that phase of his life was over: 'May 1st Ladies class *last*. Ch: rehearsal *very last*.'

Elgar left for London on 4 May for his marriage, and the dazzling career he believed to be waiting for him. For the rest of his career, Elgar wrote church music only for commission. There is only a handful of pieces, but we can be grateful that he could occasionally be tempted out of his ecclesiastical retirement, because each remaining piece dates from the period of his finest music (1897–1919), and each piece is a significant and original contribution to the *Anglican* canon of music.

1897 was the year of Elgar's next substantial piece of church music. A lot had happened to Elgar since he left St George's in 1889. He had, of course, had many setbacks in these years, including his sad (but temporary) departure from the London scene in 1891, when he considered himself a failure. However, back in the comforting surroundings of Worcestershire, he had flourished, gaining several important commissions from the Three Choirs Festivals and elsewhere. He was, by 1897, a veteran of the English oratorio scene, both sacred and secular, having completed *The Black Knight*, *The Light of Life*, *Scenes from the Saga of King Olaf* and *The Banner of St George*. Each had been received by the public and the critics with some acclaim. It was not, then, altogether a surprise when George Sinclair, the Organist and Festival conductor of Hereford Cathedral, asked Edward to write a setting of the *Te Deum* and Benedictus for the opening service of the 1897 Festival. Elgar took the opportunity to produce a grand, colourful pair of movements, not only to express the words vividly (as he always did), but also, one feels to say 'Look what I can do now! I used to play second fiddle in the Festival Orchestra, but now I command the whole affair!!' The assurance and pride of the opening theme are unmistakable.

On 5 June, Sinclair's pupil and later successor as Organist at Hereford, Percy Hull, was present when Elgar presented his new work to Sinclair. Hull wrote:

> I was privileged to hear Elgar play over his Festival *Te Deum* and Benedictus in Sinclair's house to see whether the work would be acceptable for the programme of the festival . . . He was as nervous as a kitten and heaved a huge sigh of relief when Sinclair said: 'It is *very, very* modern, but I think it will do . . .'

Elgar sent the full score to Novello, and received an excited letter from the publishing manager A. J. Jaeger, who wrote, 'I claim qualities for you which I fail to see in *all* other British composers.'

The *Te Deum* and Benedictus are happily back in the repertories of many choirs, although with the demise of the service of Matins in most British cathedrals, fewer opportunities exist for these canticles to be performed. The opening page of the *Te Deum* excited me more than anything else in those 1969 recording sessions, even though then it was played (creditably) on the organ by Harry Bramma and not by the large orchestra which Elgar intended.

Presumably, Sinclair found the work modern on account of its intense, motive-driven accompaniment and its often tortuous chromaticism. As in the preceding oratorios, Elgar adopts for these works a Wagnerian approach; that is to say, the 'action' and 'meaning' of the text are largely elucidated in the orchestra through the development of a finite number of themes. The voices articulate the words on top, sometimes almost incidentally to the main musical argument. Even the opening phrase in the voices 'We praise Thee, O God' is overshadowed by the reprise in the orchestra of the opening motive of the Prelude.

The whole of Op. 34 is characterized by an outstanding compositional technique, not only in the quality and variety of the themes and the masterly chromatic harmony, but also by often-ignored practical considerations such as the balance between the choir and the orchestra. There is always a choral–orchestral balance problem when performing in resonant Gothic cathedrals. Elgar counter-attacks by, for example, having the voices sing in unison in ff climactic passages, or by thinning the orchestration in reflective passages. Highlights are many (and personal). I particularly enjoy the triplet, syncopated ostinato which accompanies first the words 'To Thee Cherubim'; the dark, incense-filled harmony at the words 'Holy, holy, holy' and, of course, the Elgarian headlong rush to the climax at the words 'ever world without end', using helter-skelter sequences and increasingly outrageous harmony! The Benedictus is a more subdued affair, naturally, and itself has many beautiful touches, notably the soprano duet at the words 'That we being delivered . . .' The Gloria is the weakest moment in the score; of course, Elgar took the opportunity to recapitulate some of the themes from the *Te Deum*, to round off a neat cyclical form; but the opening words ('Glory be to the Father . . .') are set in a manner worthy of Walmisley or Smart. At least Elgar could be seen to have, musically at least, crossed to the Anglican side of the religious divide!

The years of the reign of King Edward VII represented the golden years of Elgar's career, and it is probably not surprising that he did not concern himself much with church music. Any religious devotion he may have had found an outlet in the magnificent series of oratorios of the years 1900–1906. It seems impossible that Elgar was irreligious, since so much of his time was spent dealing with religious subjects, which would surely have palled had he no interest in them. As he himself wrote to Delius in 1933, 'It has been a matter of no small amusement to me that . . . my name is indissolubly connected with "sacred" music . . .' However, almost all his recorded quotations on the subject of his own religious feelings betray a lack of faith; for example, this famous passage from a letter Elgar wrote to Jaeger after the failure of the first performance of *Gerontius* in 1900:

> . . . I always said God was against art and I still believe it. Anything obscene or trivial is blessed in this world and has a reward . . . I have allowed my heart to open once — it is now shut against every religious feeling . . . for ever.

There seems not to have been an outpouring of religious sentiment by Elgar even on his deathbed. He did receive the last rites of the Catholic Church, but, as Philip Leicester recorded, 'Edward [was] off his head with morphia.' Elgar did ask to be cremated and his ashes scattered at a favourite rural spot of his. This, of course, was contrary to the dogma of the Catholic Church.

My feeling is that Elgar, as a self-confessed conservative (and Conservative, as a matter of fact), respected the establishment of both the principal churches of the United Kingdom, but set religious texts as a matter of professional expediency. A strong and uncomplicated faith seems at odds with the doubts and neuroses exhibited by Elgar throughout his long life. Indeed, the state of *wanting* to believe rather than *actually* believing is to my ears audible in his music, and I am sure I am not alone in finding this in *Gerontius*.

In the Edwardian decade, then, Elgar wrote little church music that was of importance: a hymn tune, some Anglican chants, and a short anthem ('They are at rest') for the anniversary of Queen Victoria's death. However, he did write a part-song with a religious text in 1909, 'Angelus', which deserves more than a passing mention. In April of that year, Elgar and his family went to spend some weeks in Italy, primarily to assist his Muse. (His inspiration had dried up in the midst of both the Violin Concerto and the

Second Symphony.) He did not make much progress with these big pieces, but did write two charming part-songs, 'Angelus' and the ambitious 'Go song of mine'.

'Angelus' is a setting purportedly of a translation of a Tuscan religious song. It is built on an (Angelus?) bell-like ostinato in the inner parts, around which Elgar weaves an affecting and devout melody presented in parallel by the soprano and bass parts. 'Angelus' is a deceptively simple, but sincere miniature, which deserves to be better known. It is dedicated to Alice, Mrs Charles Stuart-Wortley, whom Elgar called the 'Windflower'. She was almost certainly the great love of his life.

The next time that Elgar was tempted to pen a substantial piece of church music was in 1911, by which time he had already penned most of the masterpieces for which he is best remembered and was a national figure. (He had been knighted in 1904.) For the Coronation of George V in Westminster Abbey in June, the Abbey Organist, Sir Frederick Bridge, asked Elgar to write a Coronation March and an Offertory. (In fact, Edward made a third contribution to the ceremony by recasting his *Coronation Ode* of 1902.) Shortly before the Coronation Elgar learned that he had been appointed to the Order of Merit by the King. This, the highest honour that can be bestowed in the United Kingdom should have symbolized for Elgar that he had achieved the apogee of success but for reasons that no biographer has ever managed to explain, Elgar suddenly decided not to go to the Coronation, and prevented his wife from going too, so he was not present for the performance of his new Offertory motet. Bridge had asked Elgar to set words from Psalm 5, verses 2 and 3: 'O hearken Thou unto the voice of my calling, my King, and my God: for unto Thee will I make my prayer.' These words were to be sung while the king made an offering of bread and wine for communion.

Elgar produced an exquisite masterpiece for the occasion. 'O hearken Thou' was published as Op. 64. It begins with a tender four-bar prelude, where gentle dissonances are created by converging chromatic lines over a dominant pedal. This four-bar phrase is repeated twice as an accompaniment to the voices at the end of each verse. The entry of the choir for each verse is heralded by a beautiful augmented sixth, whose scoring is redolent of the Prelude to *The Apostles* (and both movements are in A♭ major). The two verses chosen from the Psalm are treated strophically and homophonically. Verse 2 is set for a 'Verse' group, that is, reduced forces. When the full choir enters for Verse 3, the effect is magical. The harmony is deliberately opaque, almost questioning; the melody gently chromatic and evocative.

Not very many months after the performance of 'O hearken Thou', Elgar worked at a substantial setting of words from Psalm 48. He had drafted some sections of this piece back in 1910, when he was hard at work on the Violin Concerto, and all commentators draw attention to thematic similarities between the two works. The impetus for the completion of the Psalm was again an occasion at Westminster Abbey. Psalm 48 received its first performance at the service to commemorate the 250th anniversary of the Royal Society, conducted once again by Sir Frederick Bridge. Elgar described 'Great is the Lord' as 'very big stuff of Wesley length but alas! not of Wesley grandeur'. Paying homage to S. S. Wesley, Elgar indulged in the self-denigration he so enjoyed.

It begins with a long nobilmente tune for the men of the choir over an ostinato minim bass. The grandeur of this theme expresses the confidence and stability of the city of Zion, 'the city of our God'. This is followed by a brilliant passage for the upper voices to describe other aspects of Zion: '. . . beautiful in elevation, the joy of the whole earth'.

The next section (verse 3 of the Psalm) describes the 'kings of the earth' and how easily they are defeated by the forces of Zion. (Actually, Elgar does not use the words of the Prayer Book consistently in this Psalm. As in the oratorios, most notably in *The Kingdom*, Elgar used several different versions of the words of the Bible, selecting them according to his view of their literary merit, or perhaps their musical appropriateness.) This section, again built on a bass ostinato (although this time an aggressive, allegro one), gives the impression of the armies of the world on the march, and has some wonderfully vivid musical images, for example, the oscillating chromaticisms which describe the 'pain as of a woman in travail', or the terrific modulation (or shift? from C minor to B minor) which describes the 'amazement' of the doomed kings. I should add that the organ part of these pages is of unusual difficulty. A mellifluous (and very Wesleyan) bass solo (in Ab major—the rest of the piece is in D major!), a dance-like antiphonal 'Let Mount Zion be glad', and the inevitable, but nevertheless satisfying recapitulation (to the words 'For this God is our God') completes this splendid anthem in the best Anglican Tradition.

1914 was a year in which, most commentators agree, Elgar created very little of lasting artistic value. Michael Kennedy asserts that the 'potboilers' which Elgar did produce—mostly answers to requests from acquaintances—were 'the price of running Severn House' (Severn House was the Elgars' extravagant mansion in Hampstead)! Included in the list of smaller works from this year are Elgar's final two Church anthems: 'Fear not, O land' and 'Give unto the Lord', Op. 74.

'Fear not, O land' was written in the spring of 1914 and was included in the Novello Octavo Series for Church Choirs. It is a modest parish church choir type anthem and still does duty on church and cathedral music lists around Harvest Festival, when the choice of alternative pieces is extremely small. Elgar chose the words from the book of Joel, and, of course, sets them sympathetically (especially the hushed unison interpretation of the phrase 'Be not afraid, ye beasts of the field'; Elgar was sincerely fond of animals). However, he was evidently working within the strictest stylistic parameters, and the piece is almost completely devoid of musical interest. Given this, Christopher Robinson wisely omitted this piece from the 1969 recording.

It is a relief to turn to 'Give unto the Lord'. This superb work was written at the request of Sir George Martin (Organist of St Paul's Cathedral) for performance at the 1914 Festival of the Sons of the Clergy, held at St Paul's on 30 April. The certainty of this work being performed by professional musicians meant that Elgar could give a freer rein to his imagination than was the case with 'Fear not, O land'. Indeed, most writers agree that this is a finer work than its companion, 'Great is the Lord'. Certainly it is more compact, formally more satisfactory (a strict ternary form as opposed to a loose episodic form), and possibly more vivid. It begins with a marvellous, broad theme in Eb major, marked nobilmente of course! Elgar apparently had an inexhaustible fund of such themes, particularly in E♭ major—Second Symphony, *The Kingdom*, *Imperial March* and so on. This theme is effortlessly developed until a climax in the key of the flattened leading note on the word 'waters' (exciting, this—Elgar would have denied knowing what the 'flattened leading note' was! I'm not sure if I know either!). This word is accompanied by a semi-quaver flourish in the organ (or violins, depending on which version of the accompaniment is being used), which in turn leads to terrifically colourful passage where the omnipotence of God is demonstrated by various natural phenomena. The harmonic shifts on the word 'bare' are remarkable and worthy of Richard Strauss. A contemplative middle section ('In his temple doth ev'ry one speak of his honour') has a genuine feeling of awe and respect, particularly as it is in B minor—as far as it is possible to get from the home key of E♭. The modulation at the end of this passage which prepares for the musical recapitulation is as beautiful as it is sophisticated. The final pages definitely have a valedictory feel to them. Hope and nostalgia seem to be the emotions at the words 'the blessing of peace'. Within four months, the world was at war.

There is just space to mention two exquisite Christmas carols. First, 'A Christmas greeting', Op. 52, which Elgar wrote for Dr Sinclair and the Choristers of Hereford Cathedral in 1907 to words by his wife, Alice. In this charming piece, Elgar copied the scoring of the pair of much earlier upper voice songs ('Fly, singing bird, fly' and 'The snow'), i.e. the accompaniment is for piano and two solo violins. The gentle, almost sentimental flavour of the piece is enhanced by a lengthy quotation from the *Pastoral Symphony* of *The Messiah*. Secondly, 'I sing the birth' is an a cappella setting of a poem by Ben Jonson, written, it seems, long after all the rest of Elgar's religious music in 1928. It is an essay in the English modal carol style, so typical of Vaughan Williams and his followers, and surely a possible influence on Britten's much better known *A Hymn to the Virgin* (1930). There is a sincerity and naivety about this music which I find most affecting. It is light years away from the full-blown Romanticism of most of his church music, and shows that Elgar could have taken new stylistic directions had he chosen to. He need not have been locked into a compositional style which by the First World War was beginning to look rather old-fashioned.

Elgar is remembered today for his orchestral music, his oratorios and his chamber music, but not really for his church music. In the secular twenty-first century, the Church is of interest to so few that only a handful of people each year experience his church music in its liturgical setting. John Butt describes Elgar's church music as a 'small but striking oeuvre', and I hope that I have demonstrated something of the variety, colour and intelligence of this oeuvre. Fellowes and Westrup may not have thought sufficiently of it to mention any of it in their seminal work, *English Cathedral Music*; but I have been certain of its value since first singing it back in 1969.

Bibliography

The sources for the quotations used, and for all but my own personal observations and experiences, are the following well-known standard books on Elgar:

R. Anderson, *Elgar* (The Master Musicians) (London: J.M. Dent, 1993)

E. W. Atkins, *The Elgar–Atkins Friendship* (London: David and Charles, 1984)

D. Grimley and J. Rushton (eds), *The Cambridge Companion to Elgar* (Cambridge: Cambridge University Press, 2004)

M. Kennedy, *Portrait of Elgar* (Oxford: Clarendon Press, 1968)

—*The Life of Elgar* (Cambridge: Cambridge University Press 2004)

R. Monk (ed.), *Elgar Studies* (Aldershot: Scholar Press, 1990)

J. N. Moore, *Edward Elgar, A Creative Life* (London: Oxford University Press, 1984)

9

A *Sixth* Pomp and Circumstance March

ANTHONY PAYNE

Compared to the two decades I spent contemplating the sketches for Elgar's Third Symphony before I felt ready to start work on its completion, the six weeks needed to realize *Pomp and Circumstance March No. 6* came as a relief and a surprise. The March, of course, turned out to last a mere 8 minutes as against the 55-minute Symphony, but the nature of the work involved was largely similar, and the speed with which I dispatched the task had much to do with the fact that I was re-entering familiar psychological territory, that of enacting the role of another composer. This was not to be an exercise in pastiche, but composition proper.

One thing I had learned during my work on the Third Symphony was that precedents or the lack of them should not dominate one's thinking. One conductor, for instance, otherwise sympathetic to my work, had suggested that the Symphony's final cadence should be altered. 'When did Elgar ever close a work with a gong stroke?' he reasoned. My riposte was that an inspired composer is always liable to do the unexpected.

Regarding *Pomp and Circumstance No. 6*, which I saw as concluding, perhaps even celebrating, one of the most remarkable sets of short pieces in the repertory, I felt that I should re-invent the Elgarian march and not slavishly follow the practices he had so far established, leading, naturally, to the ultimate paradox, for Elgar's characteristic thinking involved not repeating himself. The variety of processes and structures found among the five marches he completed is truly remarkable. Only once did he repeat a process that had proved its worth, when in *Pomp and Circumstance No. 4* he invented a nobilmente trio melody to match the already celebrated 'Land of Hope and Glory' of No. 1. In other respects, these, the two most popular of the marches, are quite different in structure. The main section of No. 1, with its four pregnant subjects, is thematically the richest of the marches, while No. 4's is monothematic—uniquely in the set.

Nor are the expressive worlds of the five marches in any way similar to each other. No. 1 is the fiercest of them, its closest relation, No. 4, serenely majestic, while No. 2 inhabits a world of restless poetry which makes it, in the opinion of many, the most original of the set. Stanford, for instance, admired it greatly. No. 3 juxtaposes funereal and triumphal strains, while the buoyant 6/8 of No. 5's quick-march sections is offset by the most intriguing of the set's central trio melodies, a mosaic-like aggregation of phrases that builds uniquely to a grand arching statement. To bring this sequence of splendidly structured pieces to a conclusion promised to be an exhilarating and challenging task.

The whole process was launched by a phone call from Robert Montgomery, lawyer for the Elgar Will Trust, who wanted to know whether I would look at a bundle of sketches for a Sixth *Pomp and Circumstance March* and say if I thought there was enough material to make a completion possible. If so, would I do it myself? Photocopies of the sketches duly arrived by post, together with a *Musical Times* article on their provenance by the Elgar scholar Christopher Kent. A good number of them had been lying in the British Library for some years and probably would not have given me enough to go on if another small treasure trove had not come to light during the move of the Royal School of Church Music's Colles Library. It took the form of a miscellaneous group of manuscripts including three pages, clearly in Elgar's hand, marked 'P&C6'. This last and most valuable find raises the question of the dating of the sketches. The pages marked 'P&C6' probably post-date *Pomp and Circumstance No. 5*, which was completed in 1930, although this is questionable, and the other sketches are even more difficult to assign. Some are marked simply 'P&C', and could even date from the time of the first four marches, 1901–1907; while another is marked 'P&C5' but bears no relationship to No. 5 as we now know it. As for the theme marked just 'P&C', which is a more extended but obviously incomplete version of a subsidiary subject from the *Empire March* of 1924: was it a re-working of that melody's simpler phrase structure, or did Elgar raid an earlier sketch book when the Empire Exhibition commission arrived, and reduce the theme to his needs? The answer to these conundrums will probably remain a mystery, but whatever the provenance of this fascinatingly varied collection of ideas, I saw a way of welding them together, and, comforted by the composer's unpredictability, plunged in at the deep end and composed.

At the outset, however, after a casual inspection of the material, I did not find my enthusiasm whetted, and it was only after being pressed to take a second look that the penny dropped. As with the Third Symphony, I suddenly found ideas falling into place and my interest became fully engaged. The 2/4 quick march theme in G minor, found among the Colles Library sketches, just needed filling out texturally, and could launch the main section, leading to a restless and tonally ambivalent section in 6/8 found among the British Library holdings. Its highly characteristic mixture of energy and wistfulness extended for some fifty bars, but the writing was very hard to decipher, and I had to take the decision to ignore the well-nigh illegible concluding bars and bring the paragraph to a close in my own way. It is worth saying at this stage that none of the sketches is allotted a place in any notional structure by Elgar, and in none of the other P&C Marches does he combine 2/4 and 6/8 rhythms within a single section. By doing just this I felt I could help give the *March* its own unique character.

Elsewhere in the sketches was the beginning of a fine nobilmente trio, as it seemed to me, related to the *Empire March*, but developing along different and more stately lines. Elgar had broken off in mid-stream, leaving his E♭ theme in G minor, and obviously intending to bring it back to the home key with further eight-bar phrases. These I provided to complete a grandly arching cantabile.

It remains to mention two short but arresting ideas (one marked 'jolly good' by the composer) which I used to construct a patrol-like introduction over a marching tread. Again, no other *Pomp and*

Circumstance March does this. I enriched this process by foreshadowing the main 2/4 section at one point in temporarily melancholic terms. A seed is planted here that later bears fruit in fleeting moments of nostalgia, which I felt anchored the *March* in the world explored by the Third Symphony.

Part 3: Performing Elgar

10

Conducting Elgar

MARK ELDER IN CONVERSATION WITH
RICHARD MORRISON

Of all the great late Romantic symphonists, Elgar is perhaps the one whose music has travelled least well. It's rare to hear many of his major works outside Britain, apart from the *Enigma Variations* and the Cello Concerto. Even in Germany, where Elgar's reputation was strong in his lifetime, performances are comparatively rare. When Sir Charles Mackerras conducted the Berlin Philharmonic in the *Enigma Variations* in 2005, he was astonished to discover that no member of this illustrious orchestra had any memory of a previous performance.

Perhaps as a result of this continuing need for passionate advocacy, Elgar has never lacked fervent champions among the conducting profession. Hans Richter, Adrian Boult, John Barbirolli, and in more recent times such diverse personalities as Georg Solti, Yevgeny Svetlanov, Daniel Barenboim, Colin Davis and Bernard Haitink—each has found something distinctive and exciting to say in Elgar's music. But for many Elgar devotees the present-day conductor whose interpretations consistently offer the most acute insights into the music is Mark Elder, the music director of the Hallé Orchestra in Manchester. Acutely conscious of his orchestra's great Elgar traditions under Richter and Barbirolli, as well as several odd personal coincidences linking himself with the composer (he points out that their names 'virtually fit on top of each other'; that they share the same birthday, 2 June; and that they were both bassoonists in early life), Elder has embarked on an ambitious Elgar performance and recording project that has involved intense scrutiny of these teeming scores, as well as a bold revival of some performing styles commonplace in Elgar's day. As we talked in the study of Elder's Highgate home, a score of the Second Symphony —perhaps Elgar's most complex orchestral masterpiece—lay open on the desk. I began by asking Elder to give a conductor's appraisal of Elgar's character.

MARK ELDER: It's not easy to get a rounded picture of Elgar as a personality. He was very contrary, and in company he could be very difficult. He could be 'not there' even when surrounded by people who adored him. But I think you do need to get a rounded picture when you are taking on his really major works—the Violin Concerto, the Cello Concerto.

RM: I know that you came to some of Elgar's big works comparatively late in your career. Is that because you were still searching for the key to the more elusive aspects of his personality?

ME: Yes. Early on I didn't know so much about Elgar as a humorist, as a friend, as a games player and a lover of anagrams. All those things play their part in how one conducts his music. For me his personality has always been an integral part of my enjoyment of his music. My understanding grew as I learnt more and more about the tensions in his life, or about the fact that he longed to be back in the Malvern Hills even though he knew he needed a London base. Not long ago I walked on those hills and looked at that Caractacus fort, the old Roman ramparts, and felt I was at last beginning to understand something of the atmosphere that meant so much to him.

RM: And of course he was remarkably insecure for a man who had such a colossal talent and who achieved so much. That plays a large part in his music too, doesn't it?

ME: Yes, it's incredibly important for a conductor to grasp this strange quirky mixture in Elgar of inner self-belief but also of a huge neurosis about nobody understanding his music. There is so much neurosis in Elgar. He is the British Mahler.

RM: That's a very bold statement!

ME: I know. But in his amalgam of inner insecurity, his interest in large-scale forms, his writing for large orchestra, in his visionary dreaming and his use of popular musical styles, they have so much in common—though of course there are fundamental differences. Then there's the coincidence of them writing at the same time—that the crucial masterpieces in Elgar's life were written in the first years of the twentieth century, just as Mahler was giving us his greatest works.

RM: It's extraordinary to think that, as far as we know, there was no direct contact between them. They may not even have heard a note of the other's music. Obviously conductors today are very adept at capturing the neurosis in Mahler. That, in a sense, is what everybody understands it to be all about. But is Elgar's neurosis so easily captured?

ME: No. The tradition in our country is not to be so open to that, because the panoply of noise, the big tuttis which can be too brassy and veer towards pomposity and emptiness, the side of his music-making that evokes an open-top sports car whizzing along the lanes—all that is easier to hear and feel. The other stuff in between—the shimmering, uncertain harmonies, the moments of rhythmic suspension and of waiting—they are so difficult to do beautifully.

RM: There is another aspect to Elgar that has not done him any favours in the late-twentieth century, and that is his association with Edwardiana, with Empire, with pomp and circumstance. In the past I think that may have distorted people's notions of how his music should sound, as well as turning off some music-lovers altogether. Have we managed to prise Elgar free from all that baggage, so that the nuances and layers in his music can be appreciated by everyone?

ME: I don't think we are quite there yet. But that's partly because his greatest achievements won't ever be for everybody. They are too subtle and profound. There's no doubt that the general view of his personality is much broader than it was before. I think that's to do with playing the works well, which gives people a chance to find something in the music that's relevant to them now.

RM: Elgar belonged to the first generation of composers who, thanks to the invention of the gramophone, were able to pass on to posterity an exact record of how they wanted their music to sound. Even allowing for the logistical limitations of the recording process in the 1920s and early 1930s, which may have distorted Elgar's interpretations for purely practical reasons, do you find his own recordings helpful?

ME: Far more than helpful! His own conducting has been a source of great inspiration to me and many others. And those recordings are wonderful documents, not only of him and his music but also of orchestral playing at the time and of how it changed during his lifetime. I regard them as a main key to understanding his music, even though we know from contemporary reports that his interpretation was never the same from one performance to another. Take a work such as *In the South*. Only when I heard a recording of him doing the piece did I understand it. It can seem long, but Elgar solves that by going so fast in the middle of the piece that it takes your breath away. There is a devil-may-care aspect to it, and it made me realize that the structure of the piece depends on that tempo.

RM: This whole business of rubato in Elgar—the way that you pull around the tempo, so that the notes seem to ebb and flow almost in an improvisatory manner—must be a nightmare for conductors. For a start, it's largely unwritten: it has to be 'felt' by the performers. Yet it's so vital to the style, isn't it?

ME: When you listen to records of him conducting you are hugely aware of this feeling of improvisation. People always described his music-making as being very spontaneous, so much so that it sometimes made life very difficult for the players! I suppose a conductor such as Valery Gergiev has a similar quality today. It seems that Elgar never wanted to tie his own music down. He wanted it constantly to have this dreaming quality, this rhythmic freedom. The last thing he wanted was for it to be all square and clear-cut. And it was much easier in his time for music to be played like that, because musicians in the three or four generations before the microphone came along had a fluidity that my generation simply hasn't been allowed to consider. I believe that the discipline of playing for the microphone has put a blanket on rhythmic freedom.

RM: So the rhythmic freedom on Elgar's recordings is as much a product of his age as of his specific instructions to the players.

ME: Absolutely. The way that the instrumentalists play on his recordings is, I am sure, the way they played all the time in those days. Sometimes they simply seem not to respect what's been written. It's extraordinary. Yet when it's Elgar conducting his own music, I know they would be doing what he wanted. What I find so interesting is the way that some notes are played faster than they are written—they are almost thrown away—while other notes are elongated. There's a remarkable plasticity in the phrasing. If one can somehow find a contemporary way of keeping that, one should. It adds a certain whimsical quality to his music that stops it becoming heavy and square.

RM: Do you think we are too obsessed with precision now, with reproducing exactly what is on the page?

ME: I do. It's because musicians listen back so much to their own performances now. When Elgar was writing his music, he was trying to pin down his dreams, to put on paper an entire imaginative world that ranged from the heroic and the epic in the Symphonies and *Gerontius* to the lightness and the humour that he conveyed so deftly. I think that this flexibility and lightness of touch is very hard to achieve with orchestras now.

RM: If it is hard to catch this whimsicality, this continuous rubato, with British orchestras that are steeped in his music, it must be doubly so with foreign ensembles who play it so rarely. I remember Charles Mackerras telling me that when he did *Enigma Variations* with the Berlin Philharmonic, he ended up singing them virtually the whole piece to show how the phrasing should go.

ME: I can well believe it. In the rehearsal process, orchestras new to an Elgar work are trying to find their way into the notes, which can be very hard in itself. Then they need time to get used to the idiom. I believe in saying immediately to them, 'look, just linger here, push on there'. I don't hesitate; I say that straightaway. Another way in, for players new to the idiom, is to make them respect the tenuto marks. If you linger on a tenuto note, the next note must be shorter. Immediately this unlocks a door into the music's feeling, because the notes suddenly stop sounding bland and all the same. But explaining all this to, say, the Orchestre de Paris, in my best *français*, was quite a task!

RM: I suppose the converse danger occurs with British orchestras who have played Elgar so many times that the players automatically roll out a kind of 'default position' interpretation, rather than looking at the music.

ME: That's certainly a danger with *Enigma* and the Cello Concerto, and maybe the First Symphony. Not quite so much with the other pieces. In my experience, what has to be captured afresh each time is what you might call the shadow moments, the fleeting glimpses of another world that suddenly loom up and then dissipate. Both Symphonies are full of those. The first movement of No. 1, for instance, has those flowing 6/4 passages that are like shadows over someone's face—not quite sad and yet not quite happy. You need a special sound in the strings for that. I often say 'play it like French music', so that the bow moves at great speed over the string but isn't pressed hard, and the vibrato is consistent and intense. It gets more clarity that way.

RM: And there must be places where Elgar keeps orchestras and conductors on their toes by abruptly shifting mood or tempo?

ME: The opening of the fast part of the First Symphony's last movement is probably the bar I have rehearsed more than any other in his output! Coming out of the slow introduction, which is so atmospheric and gorgeous, changing the mood entirely—as if Elgar has suddenly lost his temper, or slammed a book shut—and then plunging into this restless music: it's a challenge. I'm a restless personality myself, so I understand that contrast very well. But by George, it's difficult to get an orchestra to do that together!

RM: Does his orchestration always work, or do you have to tinker with balances much? I am thinking particularly about the difficulties posed by playing his music with present-day brass instruments, when the trumpets and trombones of Elgar's day would have had much narrower bores than today's monsters.

ME: That's what I always have to remind the players. And actually most English brass players are now very sensitive and enthusiastic about this topic and about the history of their instruments. I find that trombone players, for instance, are always very interested about experimenting with the sort of trombone sound that Elgar would have heard. And there are wonderful examples of him writing low notes that would only have been possible on the

'the other Alice', Alice Stuart-Wortley—which was as intense a relationship as one can have without the two parties being lovers —was an incredibly important part of his artistic life. I think the first Alice, his wife, knew this, and never stood in the way.

RM: The 'second Alice', as you call her, was very much the opposite of the first, wasn't she?

ME: Absolutely. She was the daughter of the painter Millais, and delicate and feminine—whereas the other was very much the brigadier's daughter, very county and thick tweed skirts. This second Alice, I think, was close to being a divine aid to Elgar. They wrote to each other day after day, secretly. And the intensity of their relationship—which nearly, I sense, burst into something sexual—is enshrined in the Second Symphony, as well as *The Music Makers* and the Violin Concerto. Elgar said that in those three pieces 'I have written out my soul.' He knew that in the world in which he moved—pillar of the Establishment, Order of Merit, moustache, pomp and circumstance everywhere—he had to maintain a front of propriety. The tenderness that one senses in their relationship, which was very different from the deep love that he had for his wife, made the second Alice an inspiration for him. When he finished the first movement of the Second Symphony, he wrote immediately to her and said, 'I have just written the last note of the first movement of your symphony.'

RM: There's also that strange moment in the first movement. Elgar made an obscure reference to it as evoking something malevolent in a summer garden. Is that all tied in with this quasi-love affair?

ME: It's clear from their letters that they nearly succumbed together, but just avoided it. I think he tried to put some of the pain and the horror and the nervousness of that episode into the music, as well as the deep serenity that he found with her.

RM: It's obvious that Elgar's major works carry a huge freight of emotion, both private and public. The danger for performers, then, must be that of over-egging the pudding by adding extra, unnecessary layers of sentimentality to an already passionate score. Is there always an optimum balance in the interpretation of his music? Or are many different levels of emotional engagement possible? I recall doing a comparative study of all the different recordings of the

Cello Concerto, where the range goes from the ultra-expressionism of Jacqueline du Pré on her recording with Daniel Barenboim to the clean, almost ascetic approach of Stephen Isserlis and Yo-Yo Ma. They could exist in different musical universes.

ME: What I rehearse is the emotional narrative of these pieces. I need to make sure that this is absolutely clear to all the players, and that they, in turn, are really making the emotional language of his music understandable to the audience. That, I believe, is the performer's first and most important duty. Of course when Jackie du Pré was young, she had this incredible gift of communication and emotional openness, and astonishing musical generosity. Perhaps now one would find it over the top, a little over-egged. But her playing of that Concerto was one of the first musical things to make me cry when I was a boy. It made me realize how far music could go. I also think that there is much more feeling in his best music than tradition and the general feeling about Elgar would lead one to believe. Even in *Enigma*, which is full of brilliant humour and sleight-of-hand, there is so much delicacy of feeling. That must be made audible, even when the notes are so familiar.

RM: I see that in honour of Elgar's 150th birthday you have programmed *The Kingdom*. You have left the late oratorios till comparatively late in your own career to tackle. Do you think they are lesser works than *The Dream of Gerontius*?

ME: There's a barrier between them and me at the moment, and it is all to do with the biblical nature of the words. Not the ideas behind the piece, but the actual words. They are such long meditative texts, whereas *Gerontius* is a journey that has events and clear signposts. The 'Ordnance Survey map' of *The Kingdom* and *The Apostles* is much harder to draw, and it has kept me away from them till now.

RM: There are ritualistic elements of *The Kingdom* that are almost like a church service, aren't there? But then, that's true of *Parsifal* as well.

ME: Yes, and *Parsifal* was a major influence on Elgar. He saw it several times at Bayreuth, I believe. But the tunes in *The Kingdom* are so wonderful that, in the end, they outweigh any doubts I might have about the words.

RM: Another Elgar work to feature in your programmes in recent years—if it can indeed be called Elgar—was Anthony Payne's completion of the Third Symphony. What do you think about those unfinished fragments which Elgar left in desk drawers when he died? Do they deserve the media attention they have received?

ME: I wasn't very positive towards the Third Symphony to begin with. I was asked whether I would like to do it, and I thought, 'Hmm, I won't know the answer to that until I have done it, so I'd better say yes!' But what I loved about the experience was the sense of delving into Elgar's mind. Because Tony Payne is so humble, as well as being a brilliant man, he left a huge amount of the responsibility for bringing the score to life to the conductor. When I looked at the score for the Third Symphony in his completion, I felt a bit like Raymond Leppard all those years ago looking at Cavalli's manuscripts. You could see what the skeleton was, but you had to provide the flesh. At rehearsals, I said to Tony, 'Do you mind if I do the opposite of what you have suggested here?' And he replied, 'Not at all!' It was very collaborative and very creative. Like Mahler, Elgar's scores are full of the most incredible detail—like tiny little brush-strokes on an artist's canvas. He hardly wrote a chord without putting some expressive marking on it. There was none of that in Tony's work; he hadn't wanted to go that far. So I found myself making choices in rehearsals about how loud or soft a chord should be, or whether the notes should be legato. It was a thrillingly immediate way of testing one's understanding of what the word 'Elgarian' actually means in practice.

11

The Role of The Angel in The Dream of Gerontius

JANET BAKER

Some years ago, HRH the Princess Margaret came to see me during the interval, just before I went out to sing the role of The Angel in Westminster Abbey. We chatted for a while and then as she left the Green Room she turned at the door and said with a twinkle in her eye, 'Good luck, Janet, be an angel.'

Be an Angel, yes indeed, any role we play we have to 'be'; it has become such a part of us that, for a time, we really feel we are that person. The Angel is special and I was lucky to have the chance to play her and explore her character very deeply, through Elgar's marvellous score and the ideas expressed in Newman's wonderful poem.

It tells of Gerontius on his death bed in agony of mind, surrounded by his friends who pray for him. As his soul departs, the priest joins with them in speeding Gerontius on his way out of this world.

Part Two, where we meet the Angel for the first time, paints a completely different scene. Here, the atmosphere is peace, light; a timeless quality emerges through the music and Gerontius wakes from a sleep sensing the changes which now surround him, and gradually realizes that he is held in the arms of a mighty being, borne along at tremendous speed and listening to a wondrous sound of singing.

The voice he hears is that of his Guardian Angel who has been guiding him, watching over him all his life, and who now is carrying him towards the seat of Judgement, where he will be subjected to the unbearable glance of God; finally he will be taken by the Angel to be healed and to sleep in the waters of oblivion until she comes again to waken him.

This conversation between Gerontius and the Angel is nothing short of sublime and raises some interesting questions. Elgar, great composer that he is, has thought of everything: the performer has only to obey the markings and directions he has written on the score—these are many and one ignores them at one's peril.

Gerontius is different from the Angel: he is a human soul, newly dead; she is a being of eternity. The two singers have to make this clear. It is done for us in the music, each character having a personal tempo, and the conversation works as long as Elgar's instructions are scrupulously observed. It quite often happens that Gerontius invades the timespace of the Angel and vice versa, in which case the exchange between them loses some of its magic and shape.

Gerontius feels himself 'changed': he is refreshed, free, more himself than he has ever been. The Angel is unchanging. The important difference for her is that at last she can communicate with Gerontius directly in a way which has not been possible during his earthly life, and is able to answer the questions he wishes to ask her. She has a stillness about her and radiates joy because she knows the truth of her very first words, 'My work is done, my task is o'er', and she is taking him home. She says he is both her child and her brother; perhaps in some far-off past she has herself been human and has now attained the exalted purpose of being responsible for the welfare of another soul.

There is something very beautiful in Newman's teaching that we all have a guardian angel who is within us or beside us every step of the way. The bond between the Angel and Gerontius is significant and the thought of some force in our lives which can make us feel valued and loved is a tremendously comforting one.

Gerontius is asking many questions. 'I fain would know a maze of things', he says, 'were it but meet to ask.' She replies on the most simple, transparently written phrase, 'You cannot now cherish a wish which ought not to be wished'. Something about the triplets Elgar has written always made this phrase full of meaning for me. The whole piece has moments which I found so affecting, they are almost impossible to sing. Two pages later there is another, this time on the words, 'It is because then thou didst fear, that NOW, thou dost not fear'. The music rises to a top F sharp, and is physically exhilarating to sing.

Another example of these special moments and one which never failed to move me is the moment when Gerontius asks, 'Shall I see my dearest Master, when I reach His throne?' Elgar writes a phrase which hangs in the air, as if the phrase is too important to answer without a pause. The Angel pauses with it, and after what seems like an eternity replies 'Yes'. The one word, 'yes', has so many levels of meaning for me; the Angel knows what the sight can do to the unprepared human soul, and tells him that although he will see his Lord, he will be both gladdened and yet pierced unbearably.

All through the work it is as though the composer and poet are unified so closely that the world they inhabit becomes just that bit clearer and one is spellbound. At certain points this collaboration is lifted from an already wonderful level to an even more inspiring one. Each time one performs the piece, it is possible to find more and more of such moments because life changes us and we discover ever deeper meaning in the familiar, well-loved works we sing. It is like a journey and one of the greatest privileges the musician has.

Actors recognize this process—each time we play, special nuances, different vocal colours make for a unique, creative experience for the re-creative artist.

When one remembers how much European music has used Christian thought and liturgy, it might be difficult to understand how performers who are neither Catholic nor believers in the Christian faith can bring truth to this work.

Just as painters see the world more vividly, more significantly in terms of light than the rest of us, so musicians are affected by sound, so the starting point must always be the notes on the page of a score. If singers also develop a sensitivity for words, then these two forms of 'truth' enable them to enter the world of composer and poet to a sufficient degree that they have authenticity. Unlike any other musicians, vocalists have this singular benefit of a two-pronged basis which the music and words give them.

Newman's poem has different levels. The outer and most imme-diately accessible is the story which is based on Catholic doctrine;

but the story can be seen in a wider sense, in that the journey of Gerontius is one we all undergo. The trials, the agony, his death-bed distress of conscience are all trials we understand and share in some measure. The idea of a companion who loves us unconditionally, who will be there to guide us both in this life and, hopefully, in the next, strikes a chord in the heart of many people.

The performer needs to play many parts in the course of a career and try to enter into them all. There can be no more inspiring and compassionate role than that of the Angel; it is difficult to judge in this work, which is the most important influence—the music or the ideas which are expressed through it.

The greatest challenge awaiting any singer is the resolution of the constant battle between words and music which rages within every work we approach. If the composer is of the first rank the decision is, to a great extent, made for us, but every so often we are given a certain leeway where the boundaries of the musical phrase give way and present us with a kind of freedom. This is where the performer shows his stature, choosing for himself which precise word is to be stressed and the depth of meaning it will be given—all will depend on the individual's personal understanding and intelligence.

Years ago, the fully trained singer in 'bel canto' was weighed by the audience in such moments and judged accordingly. To articulate words clearly without disturbing a beautiful sound and to invest supreme meaning to them equally is the highest art to which any singer can aspire.

There are all sorts of tricks to be learned using the organs of articulation in the face, a skill undervalued today when even ordinary speech of every day is slovenly, lazy and difficult to understand. But for the few students who are willing to do the colossal and never-ending work involved, there are great secrets to uncover and the powers of interpretation can rise to immeasurable heights.

I can't begin to count the number of times a stranger has stopped me in the street to say how much this work has meant to them or a member of their family in times of trouble.

There is deep power of comfort and hope in *The Dream*, which reaches out beyond the outward expression of Newman's poem and Elgar's music and satisfies a need in the human heart. We all, performers and audience alike, touch the fringes of something indescribable and inexplicable, and find ourselves able, for a little while at least, to face the world.

For a moment the power of music allied to the power of words is placed in the hands of the singer as the medium between composer, poet and audience, bringing with it the most awesome responsibility and the most sublime joy.

12

Sir Edward Elgar: My Musical Grandfather

YEHUDI MENUHIN

For me, the Elgar violin concerto will always hold more meaning than a purely musical one, in that it evokes a less universal and more specific atmosphere, one composed of people I love, of places which evoke the roots of my life, a youthful atmosphere of time which must appear to most of us illuminated by nostalgic candle-light compared with the inhuman and merciless glare of contemporary life.

This particular association is surely not just my own, for I feel I share it with the British people and with those of my own generation who hear this music in the same spirit of comfortable surrender as when one settles into the consoling and familiar folds of a beloved armchair.

I well remember the sunny day when I first made my acquaintance with the infinitely shaded green of an English summer and with Sir Edward who, to me, symbolized in one way the country I had come to love.

I was 16 years of age when we met in an hotel room where HMV had already arranged for Mr Ivor Newton to play the piano reduction for me as accompaniment. I played a few bars in a mood at once eager and anxious, for I had just prepared the work and I was, after all, presenting it to the composer himself.

I had scarcely reached the end of the first page when Sir Edward interrupted, assuring me that he had no qualms about the performance, he was sure the recording would be excellent, and—as for him—he was off to the races.

I was terribly impressed, as I had never met so trusting and casual a composer. Of course, I came to realize how much lay behind this cultivated air of detachment, indeed how much warmth, feeling and intensity were at work within the unruffled frame of all the English, both individually and collectively.

It was therefore of particular sentiment to me that HMV should choose to commemorate the 100th anniversary of Elgar's birth by bringing out anew on a long-play record this version of the violin concerto recorded in my mid-teens with Sir Edward.

I really feel it would be redundant of me to dissect the work or to discuss it technically for the benefit of the English public. Is it not sufficient to say that, for me, it presents something so intrinsically English in its charm and persuasive, lyrical beauty that, as I felt in those far-off days with Elgar, this music is a language we share, one that needed then no especial translation between himself and myself, any more than it does now between myself and the English audience.

For me, it is the vocal expression of a bond that I have felt since I first played with them and, as such, is more articulate than any words I might find to explain it.

I had not yet lived in England, and all these qualities I intuitively sensed in the score and the sound. Already the 'feel' of the music, flow-surge and Brahmsian warmth, already Enesco's words, commenting on the melody, intrigued and puzzled me—for I knew I was holding the key to the very heart of a people; the music which would reveal their deepest consciousness and unselfconsciousness to me; the music which would assure them I understood and loved them. In a curious way, other great composers had already dissociated themselves from, and sublimated their direct bonds with, their own people—but, at least in 1932, Elgar was still contemporary with the ethos, the Geist, the deepest wells of being of the vast majority of his people. It was still to be a few years before I played Bach to what must be the last surviving pocket of fervent, passionate and uncompromising Protestant congregations at the Munster in Basel—so compelling and overwhelming a condition that I knew, had I transgressed an iota with too wide a vibrato, let alone a slide, I would be forever damned or, even more likely, instantly condemned to the hideous fate of that illustrious forebear of mine, of which there were in evidence a number of stern factual reminders hanging about.

As for Mozart, I shall never play his music for those courtly, chivalrous, conventional, elegant yet ritualistically abandoned audiences to which it was addressed; yet, in a totally different age, these, his qualities, are valid, the apparently ephemeral delicacy of inflection and gesture as potent and moving—at least in England and our Europe—as in Mozart's day. Again, it was still to be some eighteen years before I played Brahms in Hamburg and Bremen—to those Hanseatic people who know the timelessness of a shrouding mist and the corresponding values of humanly generated warmth and cosiness. I had not yet played Nielsen or Grieg in Scandinavia, Bartok in Budapest, Enesco in Bucharest or Bloch in Israel. Paganini in Rome seemed to correspond a shade more than Lalo in Paris—although obviously Italian and French respectively, neither composer's identification with his people was as deep or exclusive as the aforementioned. Obviously, folk music coincides with a people's way of being. Scottish reels on bagpipes or fiddle, gypsy airs on zither or violin, the Greek shepherd's flute or the Viennese waltzes of Strauss—all a halfway mark between musique folklorique and musique savante.

What was it that Enesco had actually meant when he said this melody of Elgar's was so typically, so characteristically, English? I felt it in my very bones, and I was at one with the quality—yet it took me many years, and only after I had myself been shorn of something of that selfsame pristine sheen, before I was able to define it as an unashamed ecstatic innocence. Elgar's voice is not one of prophetic warning, neither is it a solemn sermon; it is not deliberately or self-consciously brutal, neither aggressive nor repentant—for it is unconscious of guilt or evil. It does not speak of desperation, or of the colossal, symbolic, swollen Teutonic world of Wagnerian mythology; it does not even speak of unrequited love or of the fear of self—Schubert's Doppelganger is a far cry. It is unashamed not because it has overcome shame and is brazen, but simply because it never had to. It is as it is.

It is simply because the Englishman is complete, as a plant or a tree is complete. How far have the great English qualities been

debased and violated today? Let us hope that the modern archi-
tecture, the politics, the vulgarity and the fragmentation of ideals
and ambitions represent merely the passing phase, a phase associated with a world of noise, shouting, competition and immediate
reward or penalty. I feel it must be so; that the qualities which I love
and recognize as English qualities continue to imbue many of the
young people I know and are still in evidence, however much they
are attacked and spurned. I feel there must be a basic, racial,
national character of which Elgar himself, who loved the human
voice, the violin, and those sympathies were withheld even from the
piano—that useful, mechanical instrument—is proof for me of the
eternal English qualities which I would like to think are incor-
ruptible.

In his music there is the same openness, directness and simplicity
which blessed so many Englishmen with that self-evident pragmatic
approach—the approach which eschewed dogmas, theories, 'sys-
tems' or inelastic philosophies; that approach which revealed the
evolutionary pattern to Darwin, the mystery and poetry of the
Antarctic and its life to Wilson, the impressionistic revelations to
Turner, the sensual and mystical sides of John Donne. It seems to be
a natural subtraction of the self; of that self which, with wilfulness
and prejudice, would bend creation to its own will, or would justify
such in the name of dogma or theory. In no nation is the poetic, the
metaphysical and the scientific so inextricably blended as in the
English.

As I sensed at our first encounter that summer's afternoon, here
was not a self-conscious composer, a labelled specialist, as was the
case with other composers I had met, after the manner of that
bearded Old Testament prophet Bloch, or the intellectually ascetic
Ravel; here was a natural phenomenon, indigenous to the land
—simply the largest, oldest, most beautiful and sheltering oak tree
around which the countrymen danced and which, in a very friendly
way, without fear or trembling, they worshipped. The Druids had
not entirely disappeared.

Those beautiful, beckoning horses, irresistibly compelling his
presence at the races were, I felt, of basic concern to Sir Edward
and, although at first admittedly mystified, I soon understood why
it was rightly so, why of commensurate significance or perhaps of

more immediate importance than the ultimate recording of the violin concerto on the Wednesday and Thursday.

I never did enquire whether Sir Edward won or lost on the horses that afternoon. Thus do gentlemen compose, win wars, solve problems; thus do they govern; thus do they submit to government, and I recognized it all—for with the same kind of approach did my mother insist I should be a violinist, so a violinist I had to be—a blend of utter devotion with almost casual carelessness.

This dedication, commitment, zeal, work, seriousness, but also humour, taking precedence in my life and my career, meant we were serving quite simply and unaffectedly a natural order, a natural obligation greater than ourselves—as does the ant, the oak tree, the hummingbird or the whale.

Of course, contrary to God's injunction, I did work on the intervening day—I had thought it was a Sunday. However, already imbued with the English dharma, and following a family custom established since my sister's and my own earliest infancy, my father and I walked the length and breadth of Hyde Park with its grazing sheep and its Serpentine—at the time the one authentic peninsula of English countryside penetrating into the very heart of the metropolis, with no high-rise monstrosities to mar that so perfect and so English vision and conception. I could not yet know until my next and unforgettable lovely summer days in London, only thirteen years later, that the gathering storm would have burst upon my beloved England and Europe, bringing untold pain and destruction, and that a marriage, still quite undreamt of, would have already collapsed—and that in 1945 I would, in this very London, be embarked upon the happiest, richest, most fulfilling part of my life, still continuing now, thirty years later, with my darling Diana already by my side.

But then at least came Wednesday morning. But not before another, and less glorious, 'first' took place. At lunch, the head waiter at Grosvenor House most politely yet firmly obliged me to return to our suite and attire myself properly with jacket and tie before I could enjoy those marvellous trolleys of freshly stewed fruit and all those enticing puddings and custards. As you can see, my training as an honorary Englishman goes back nearly half a century, and perhaps my playing at the studios of HMV and EMI was as effective an English formation as might have been any playing upon the fields of Eton.

It was to take place at studio number 1 at Abbey Road, still HMV, not yet EMI, the dog still very much in evidence—a room I have used for some 45 years which, despite its innumerable reincarnations with each superseding of one recording technique by another, has always retained for me its first friendliness and homeliness. There was Fred Gaisberg, whose brainchild the project was, waiting smilingly—Sir Edward, altogether benign and happy —and the biggest orchestra I have ever played with; the great composer himself in charge, conducting his own work; the atmosphere as relaxed and happy as if we were going to celebrate a feast—and that is indeed what did take place.

No violin concerto I had ever played embodies so luxuriant and colourful an orchestral sound. I was overwhelmed with the beauty, warmth and generosity of that sound, which seemed automatically to be translated into the very same human qualities. Again, that organic quality which proscribes any violation of a given order and which is the antithesis of any over-assertion, be it a conductor's or a dictator's, held sway—I had never seen a conductor do so little. His presence—a few discreet indications and the sound swelled, the pace flexible and yielding, the attack brilliant, incisive; only one specific request do I remember, five bars before first solo and after number 8 (second theme at 16), which Sir Edward wanted louder and grander.

It is a pity not to have a recording of Kreisler but, apart from the Sammons, I have one by Heifetz and two of my own: the one with Sir Edward, 1932, and the one with Sir Adrian Boult, nearly three decades later, the making of which afforded me much pleasure, for Adrian is root and branch of that very English growth to which I have alluded, so that we travelled easily together through that same countryside—I hope he felt as I did—conversing in the same tongue, even perhaps with something approaching the same accent. The Sargent/Heifetz recording has a rather stiff and martial beginning although Heifetz himself is always brilliant and masterly: there is, if I may say so in all humility, too much which is striving after effect, for attention to detail must be a means to an end and not an end in itself and in no composer is it more essential to bear this in mind than in the works of Elgar—a great naturalist if ever that term could be applied to music. Henry Wood/Sammons is touching, natural, no doubt nearer to the way Kreisler would have played it, although I find Sir Henry Wood's opening terribly fast. In listening to my own, I feel a greater affinity with Albert Sammons' spirit and for that I am thankful.

I was enthralled by his music, of which the emotion, infinitely accommodating to successive impulses, reflected that typical Ruskinesque, William Morris fascination with living, natural shapes. There is hardly a four-bar stretch, and often even within half-bars, which remains immune to the palpitation of ebb and flow; only in specific passages, in deliberate contrast to the great flow of the work, is a more or less strict metronomic sequence called for. I was naturally acquainted with the free improvisational mood, or again, in a solo voice, the almost erratic but sanctioned abandon of the coloratura aria, accompanied by compliant and subservient gentlemen in the pit—but I had never known a great orchestra respond as one man and so sensitively and unerringly to such myriad intertwining fluctuations. This is the mark of the amazing Englishness of the English—that, at the very height of Victorian grandiloquence their greatest composer retained the fluidity, the flexibility, the total absence of aggressive uniformity of discipline of his noblest forebears Purcell and Dowland.

Playing this intoxicating music, I was not interpreting a man's 'impression' of a garden; I was, much more, expressing the nature of each plant, each view—I felt a oneness with nature, and human nature, which I have not known with any other composer. Whereas in Mozart each group of notes is a gesture, with Elgar it is an ephemeral state of being constantly in flux yet never going to extremes, neither moodily self-indulgent, nor aggressively and ruthlessly self-assertive. It is music which allows the player and the listener time in which observation and sympathy can weave those bonds which attach the Englishman as much to his garden and his animals as to his fellow men.

A new world of music had opened to me on that Wednesday and Thursday—a new world of gentle, all-embracing humanity—and Elgar himself acquired a humane role in my family. Having known no grandparents, the role of benign ancestor was vacant and waiting for the suitable candidate.

During the autumn following our recording came that, for me, unforgettable November concert in London when Sir Thomas Beecham and Elgar both accompanied me in two (or was it three?) concertos at the Albert Hall. With Beecham I played one of the D major concerti, no. 4 or 7 I believe, and also possibly a Bach; and with Sir Edward the concerto. As I remember, at that time Beecham was still nimble enough to stand on his own feet but Sir Edward used a red velvet upholstered bench and balustrade, but only to lean on, not to sit on.

However deeply and introspectively I felt about Elgar and the concerto, my experience of his music and his Englishness has been subjective, intuitive and confined to the laboratory atmosphere of a recording studio. Now, at last, the London public, and that best of all publics, my beloved Albert Hall audience would corroborate, or not, my interpretation of Elgar. I did not read, nor do I remember any comment on, the concert reviews, both erudite and journalistic: my concern is and was with the living moment, not its dissection.

Suffice it to say, we all held each other in one long embrace, for we had shared secrets, we had exchanged confidences which I am bold enough to say continue a mutual devotion unabated to this very day.

Of course you can understand how eager I was to reveal to the French, my first Europeans, whom I came to know in 1927 when I was 11, this my deepened understanding and love of Elgar, the English and England. Elgar himself had some misgivings—but when Enesco himself, beloved of the Parisian musical public, agreed to carry the proselytizing burden with me, I knew there would be at least no danger of overt hostility.

I do not have the letters between my parents and Sir Edward —but such were the bonds that attached us to each other, musical and human, that when I decided to share my new and passionate enthusiasm with my Paris audience and my colleagues in France, those very individualistic orchestral musicians of France, it came as a natural sequence that Sir Edward should visit us at Ville d'Avray in the Parisian banlieue, abutting on the Parc de St Cloud on the Eastern side of Paris across the Seine, just beyond the Bois de

Boulogne and the racecourse of the Longchamps. It was heart-warming for us children to see our mother, for once (the only time, alas, as we had no grandparents) more solicitous of an older generation than of the younger. Sir Edward's only hesitancy concerned the special diet that his ulcers required. My mother assured him that this would in no way be a burden for the household — and in an excess of zeal, Sir Edward received onion soup for breakfast. Fred Gaisberg, who accompanied Sir Edward to Paris, remained in the metropolis, somewhat reluctantly abandoning the master to our care.

It must have been the late spring of the year following the recording, May 1933, for the weather was sunny and even onion soup for breakfast could be taken out of doors on the wisteria-hung veranda, that this reconciliation took place. Long before the European Community and its exigencies of decorous distrust, and only barely 100 years since Waterloo, and decades before the British Council embarked on its official efforts to sponsor British artists, many of my French friends felt I was somewhat quixotic and foolhardy.

My beloved master Enesco took two full rehearsals to prepare the Elgar concerto ahead for Sir Edward's own casual run-through on the morning of the concert. Such was Enesco's understanding, thoroughness and authority, the feared and often unjustly maligned French musicians behaved as lambs and played beautifully. Sir Edward himself was tremendously impressed and supremely grateful to Enesco and told him so. If I remember rightly, Enesco came back to lunch at Ville d'Avray after the rehearsal.

It would be interesting to know if France had ever heard any work of Elgar's and if this performance was not in fact Elgar's 'premiere audition'. Be that as it may, French respect for old age, as symbolized in this venerable, white-moustachioed Britisher; the obvious devotion, dedication and enthusiasm of their own musicians on stage, not to speak of Enesco's and my own conviction; the sheer sonorous mass in time, volume and space (the French have a perverse and masochistic reverence for any piece of music which requires over two horns: Wagner, Bruckner, Mahler; Brahms is too short); and perhaps in a few cases, last and least the music itself, contrived to accord the work a warm and friendly reception. It has, however, never been played since in Paris, or, presumably, anywhere else in France.

It may be time to repeat the experience—for I hold the tenet that certain worthy efforts, with no regard for success or recompense, should be tried as a matter of principle every fifty years.

During his stay, Elgar went off in the direction of Fontainebleau for a long day's visit to Delius. I wish I had begged to accompany him. It would have been unforgettable to see these two aged Englishmen together.

Times have changed however. Already, during the war Anglo-American devotion extended to a performance of the concerto I gave with Sir Malcolm Sargent conducting the NBC orchestra in New York. But, quite on its own merits and appeal, the music of Sir Edward and in particular my beloved concerto has become an ever more requested and gratefully received work to play to American, and, of course, Canadian audiences. New York, Indianapolis, Winnipeg, etc. have responded to and enjoyed it.

I am particularly curious about German audiences. Although Elgar is so totally different from Brahms, there is sufficient affinity of warmth, generosity and the romantic for one to be able to hope for a very enthusiastic reception. I know Barbirolli had great success with Elgar in Berlin. I must invite one of the brilliant, younger British conductors to do it with me in Berlin or, perhaps, if a British orchestra should go on a German or Chinese tour, with all that lies between, the British Council might consider the Elgar Concerto not too great a gamble.

There were so many bonds which held us in our close friendship, perhaps not the least of which was Elgar's real understanding of the violin. He was in fact a violinist and he once gave me an ingenious étude he had composed. No doubt he was infected by a touch of that healthy vulgarity which is the hallmark of almost every violinist. It is so organic and melodic as an instrument that perhaps violinists might be forgiven, as are tenors and sopranos, for this self-indulgence. This side of Elgar, however, belonged to the European era and not specifically to England. I would like to illustrate this epoch to which England belonged by comparing Vienna's 'Schön Rosmarin' and 'Caprice Viennois' with Elgar's 'Salut d'Amour' and 'Capricieuse'.

It was the period of the European 'salon', when romanticism had become domesticated, when the chivalrous had given way to the galante. Perhaps the most popular form of this devolution is tea music or 'le fiv'-o'clock', as the French call it. Although it is an English institution, on the Continent it has usually been accompanied by music, whereas in England it was conversation rather which marked the tea period and, for this reason, it is perhaps difficult to place Elgar's Madame or Madamoiselle Capricieuse in English life.

The fascinating fact about Elgar's Englishness is that, however much he belonged to the era of grandiloquence, elegance, pomp and circumstance, he retained an Englishness which remained above and beyond these passing fashions, a nobility and a generosity, a humour and a modesty which shine through his greatest music.

13

The Violin Concerto

TASMIN LITTLE

I will never forget the impact of hearing the Elgar Violin Concerto in concert for the first time. I was in my late teens and, bearing in mind the fact that I had studied for ten years at the Yehudi Menuhin School, I now find it strange that I had not been aware of the piece before. Yehudi Menuhin was one of the Concerto's greatest champions and the impact of his recording was monumental. However, it is fair to say that there was a period from the 1970s to the 1990s when the piece was not frequently performed in the concert hall, and it did not receive anything like the attention that it commands at the present time. Even now, although most performing violinists are aware of this great work, there are still too few who have it in their repertoire—so there is a way to go yet before it is on a par with the Bruch and Brahms concertos as 'standard repertoire'.

When I first got to know the Elgar Concerto, I wondered why the piece was not more often heard. The answer became all too clear when I began to study and perform it at the age of 22.

For a start, there is the issue of the great length of the work. In some performances on disc, such as Albert Sammons', the Concerto lasts approximately 45 minutes, and this is the shortest performance that I know of; in others, such as Nigel Kennedy's, the duration can be up to one hour. That is a huge length of time to sustain a violin concerto, and no other major violin work can match it in terms of scale. Even the Beethoven and Brahms concertos, which are the next longest, rarely run longer than 40 minutes; and the Sibelius, which is also considered 'heavyweight', is nearer half an hour.

Given this huge canvas, one of the biggest challenges lies in shaping the work and in physically maintaining one's stamina in performance, not to mention sustaining audience interest throughout. In addition to maintaining one's energy, the technical difficulties are extremely demanding. Elgar knew how to write for the violin in a way that few other composers can, but he left no physical stone unturned in this powerful tour de force. It is scored for full symphony orchestra and the strength of the writing is often the way the orchestra is used at full tilt alongside the soloist. Therefore, not only does the solo violinist need to feel on top of the technical and stamina demands, but one is also aware of the need to project every note adequately in order simply to be heard. This is particularly tricky in the quieter passages, as one wants to convey an intimate feeling whilst still remaining audible, so the balance with the orchestra is crucial.

A further problem to solve lies in the matter of the standard of orchestra—just as Elgar makes no allowances for the soloist's technical difficulties, so it is for the orchestra. Some of the tuttis are astonishingly virtuosic, particularly when taken at breakneck speed, such as in the 1929 Sammons/Henry Wood performance on disc. Add to that the fact that this Concerto ranks among the hardest for a conductor to accompany and one can realize how there may have been a certain reluctance—or simply lack of rehearsal time—to programme the piece. The accompanied cadenza is somewhat notorious in musical circles for those conductors who have had experience with the work.

Finally there is the problem of where to place the Concerto in a concert performance. There are three potential ways of dealing with this. If a conservative average duration is approximately 50 minutes, one can place the work on its own in the first half of the concert. Personally, I do not favour this, as it is not easy for an audience to launch straight into listening to this great work at the very beginning of a concert. If one agrees that the Concerto is best heard by an audience who have settled down and 'warmed up', then one has only two other options. The first is to put an overture beforehand and risk the audience's powers of concentration waning as the duration of the first half tops one hour. Or one can solve the problem by simply placing the Concerto on its own as an entire second half. This is the place I most prefer, bearing in mind that it is akin to a 'symphony with soloist'.

The Concerto is both lengthy and unusual in its structure and the single most inspired deviation from traditional form is in Elgar's use of the now famous *accompanied cadenza*. To have a cadenza *with* accompaniment is rare enough, but even more extraordinary is the musical positioning of this cadenza. In most violin concertos, the cadenza is situated near the end of the first movement, before a coda or final tutti. However, Elgar chooses to place the accompanied cadenza at the very end of the Finale, just at the moment when one is expecting a 'straightforward and triumphant ride home'. Time and momentum temporarily stop as the ghostly mood of 'thrummed' strings and filigree violin detail improvises and meanders its way to a conclusion—and, ultimately to the conclusion of the Concerto. It is this which sets the Elgar Violin Concerto apart from all others; so the next question is, why did Elgar choose to place his cadenza in this most unusual position? In order to answer this, I believe we must delve briefly into the emotional idea behind the Concerto.

Some people, myself included, believe that the answer to the spiritual concept which shapes the work lies in the Spanish inscription which is found at the beginning of the score:

Aqui esta encerada el alma de.....

Which, roughly translated, means:

herein is enshrined the soul of.....

Who is signified by these five dots?

It has been suggested that it is Elgar's own name which is implied; however I believe that it signifies a woman, and very probably Alice Stuart-Wortley. She was something of a muse for Elgar and he always referred to her as 'Windflower', which also implies that he felt there was an elusive quality about her. When the inscription was first written down, Elgar used the preposition del', which implies that the first letter of the next word is a vowel. Later he changed it to 'de' in order to give less of a clue as to the identity, but he admitted to a close friend that the soul was a feminine one. Certainly the whole feeling behind the work is one of yearning, and it was Alice Stuart-Wortley who urged Elgar on when he was having difficulty composing the work. He strongly associated her with the Concerto and, during the lengthy correspondence that occurred between the two at the time, he always referred to the piece as 'your concerto'. For me, the answer lies in part of a letter that he wrote to her: 'My dear Windflower, you will be conducting the concerto, wherever you are.'

Musically speaking, the whole Concerto is like a monumental journey in search of something elusive, and it is not until the accompanied cadenza that the answers, as well as resignation to the emotions, are found. As soon as this catharsis is complete, the music takes on a triumphant and even jolly character! The whole way that the Concerto ends feels light-hearted, as though a great weight has been lifted and the solution has been found. It is likely that we will never know the true identity of the mysterious soul, but perhaps it is the constant questioning which gives the Concerto such an elusive feeling.

In preparing the piece, I always go back to the score, as there are a great many markings. Elgar is so descriptive about exactly how each note should be played, using accents, lines and tenuto markings above almost every note. It would certainly be easier to take the quick route and simply learn how to play all notes. But, if you ignore the markings, the piece can become either unintelligible or devoid of momentum. The solution is to take each marking on board but to treat it as a 'written-out improvisation'. Not every single pause *has* to be the same length. Nor need every accelerando be too gradual. Some tenuti are longer than others; and some accents are forceful while others must surely be expressive. The musical line must flow apparently effortlessly, and the destination of the phrase and the structure of each movement must always be in the forefront of one's mind. If this is achieved then, even if more time is taken during a phrase, the sense of the musical thought remains obvious.

I love the opening of this Concerto possibly more than any other. Elgar doesn't hesitate to take us in to the very centre of the fray and this opening tutti is almost like a précis of the whole movement.

When the orchestra has offered up each theme in turn and it is the soloist's turn to enter, the first solo note and the chord underneath it feel like the completion *and* the beginning of the movement. In his characteristic way, Elgar is using the violin both alongside the orchestra and as a separate entity. The first movement is the most impetuous in character and although there are moments of reflection, such as the gentle and wistful second subject, even these passages have a feeling of underlying momentum.

The gentle simplicity with which the second movement begins is a perfect antidote to the drama of the previous movement, and the writing is beautifully lyrical although it also becomes passionate. There is a quotation above the second subject of this movement which says 'Where love and faith meet, there will be light' and it is this which Elgar wanted inscribed on his tombstone. This is such an overwhelming climax, and is also the place where my favourite command occurs: 'Vibrato!' Needless to say, this request is completely unnecessary as it would be virtually impossible to be a musical and sensitive performer and *not* wish to vibrate at that wonderful moment! However, it is quite obvious how personal this work was for him and how much passion he felt for the person to whom it was spiritually dedicated.

The final movement is unquestionably the hardest. By this time one has been on the concert platform, playing at full tilt, for approximately twenty-five minutes — and the most difficult technical and musical demands have not yet begun! The scale and sheer amount of notes in this movement have led some performers to make a cut mid-movement. Henry Wood was the first to use the cut in a 1916 recording for Columbia; and Elgar himself allowed Marie Hall to make the cut in their 1916 recording for the Gramophone Company. However, I do not believe that this cut works; and providing one keeps the tempo moving, the musical line is completely sustainable. There are very few tuttis and moments of rest for the soloist in this movement, but the pacing is critical. The faster one keeps the earlier sections of the movement, the greater the impact of the cadenza. It is that wonderful moment when the entire thrust of the work is suspended which is the moment that I will never forget when I first heard it live. I had been quite convinced that the Concerto was homeward bound — not a bit of it! There is a further reason why it is important to keep the line moving beforehand, which is that it enables one to have even more sense of freedom and improvisation in the cadenza. The effect can be breathtaking. When the orchestra pauses briefly to allow the soloist to play a few bars entirely alone, this seems to be the most intimate moment of reflection; and when they return for the final, resigned offering of the *idée fixe* phrase which opens the whole piece, this is the crucial turning point for the music. From then onwards, the past is over and the future looks secure. No more backward glances.

To date, I have given nearly fifty performances of the Elgar Violin Concerto, mostly in the United Kingdom, but also abroad in Slovenia, Australia, New Zealand, Venezuela and the Far East.

I generally favour brisk tempi, as it keeps a sense of flow and also allows a feeling of impetuousness, which is a characteristic that goes well with Elgar's music. He must have liked his music taken with passion and abandon, as Lady Elgar recorded his views after one performance in 1911 with Henry Wood conducting: 'It was not well conducted—points made & phrases dragged out sentimentally, not the right reading.' Perhaps she and Elgar made their feelings known to him, because, by the time Wood recorded it in 1929 with Albert Sammons, the tuttis went like the wind!

One of the interesting things about performing the piece abroad is the different approaches and attitudes of non-English conductors and orchestras who may not be familiar with the work. I am not always in favour of certain traditions associated with this Concerto, and there are some places where, for instance, it is the 'done thing' for an English orchestra to take a step backwards in tempo; often it is not written in the score and I prefer to keep the momentum, so I always need to rehearse these places several times in order to try to 'overwrite' the natural tendency of the orchestra to play it the way they are used to. One often finds these habits occur when a particular conductor has insisted many times on a certain phrase being performed exactly one way.

Consequently there can be a freshness about going outside the UK and shaking off all preconceptions. This was most obvious when I went to perform the work in Venezuela some years ago. Having got up at 4a.m. to take a flight from Maracaibo to Caracas, the first rehearsal began at 7a.m. We were all sleepy; however the apathy from the orchestra was born out of a misconception that this was going to be 'slow, dull, lengthy and passionless English music'. The entire string section were only one step away from being horizontal on their chairs and something had to be done fast! I took matters firmly into my hands and by the end of the exposition section, having achieved a very successful Allegro molto tempo, the whole string section were sitting bolt upright, playing as if their lives depended on it! Needless to say, by the time we had sprinted our way through the first movement, their new attitude and sense of excitement at the work were reflected in their smiling faces and an obvious sense of relief. To this day I remember the performance well, as being one where the fiery South American temperament joined British passion and created a unique blend of adventure and excitement.

However, there is something undeniably special about the innate understanding that British orchestras have for Elgar's music. This is the result of many years' collective experience, and is not something that can be attained overnight. I have many wonderful memories of UK performances of the Concerto; but the performance which I remember above all others took place at the Three Choirs Festival in 1998 at Gloucester Cathedral. Richard Hickox and the Philharmonia Orchestra were my musical partners on stage and something quite extraordinary happened that evening. The rehearsals had certainly gone well and the performance itself took off in a magical way. Early on in the first movement I began to experience something that I had never felt before on stage and has never happened to me since. It felt like I was strangely out of control of my body and that an outside force was moving my arms and hands for me. I was playing and yet I was making no effort or endeavour to do so. I need hardly add that this is a bizarre circumstance to find oneself in during a piece of such difficulty; and yet I wasn't remotely worried. I simply had this wonderful feeling that everything was working exactly as it should and I didn't have to do anything at all, except to allow myself to be a vehicle for the performance. It was possibly the best rendition of it that I have ever given. But I could never have predicted the amazing ovation that the audience would give me, nor did I expect that they themselves would have felt that something highly unusual had happened that night. I had felt that the spirit of Elgar was actually present in the Cathedral, and I am not normally quick to entertain feelings of the supernatural. However, after the performance I lost count of the people who independently came up to me and said that they had felt Elgar's presence in the building. Many people were visibly moved, some were surprised and even shaken—but they all felt that they had had an intangible experience.

For me, this Concerto is a journey unlike any other concerto, an intensely personal work of deep spirituality and love. Elgar must have felt so himself as he wrote, 'I know the feeling is human and right.' From the first chords of the orchestra and the searching rise and fall of the opening theme which will make itself felt throughout the piece, one is aware of the first steps of a long road—a sense of moving eternally forward to find the answer which cannot be fully understood until the intricate workings of the accompanied cadenza have played themselves out. And although I know this work so well and have studied the score so many times, I never feel that I have found everything that there is to express. Like all truly great works, there is always a further musical challenge to resolve and more beautiful details to find in this great and truly moving Violin Concerto.

14

The Cello Concerto—Jacqueline du Pré's Recordings

ANDREW KEENER

She's playing it rather well, and looks likely to be my successor if she carries on.

Grand words from the first grande dame of Elgar's Cello Concerto, Beatrice Harrison, 68, and long retired to the tranquility of her Surrey cottage. It was 1960, the Elgar scholar Jerrold Northrop Moore was her confidant, and in one sweep the work's gramophonic creator seems, on the face of it, to be dismissing the three decades of recorded performances which followed her pioneering discs of 1919 and 1928 under the composer's baton. The first, W. H. Squire's 1930 78rpm discs with Sir Hamilton Harty conducting the Hallé Orchestra, is the work of a fine chamber musician to whom an admiring Fauré had dedicated his *Sicilienne*. Next, in the mid-1940s, came Pablo Casals with Sir Adrian Boult and the BBC Symphony Orchestra, re-evoking in peacetime the solace which the great Catalan cellist's London performance had brought to concert-goers in the troubled years before the Second World War. By the end of the 1950s—the first vinyl decade—three more soloists had committed celebrated interpretations to disc: the Frenchmen Paul Tortelier and André Navarra (with Sargent and Barbirolli respectively), and Anthony Pini, distinctive on gut strings, conducted by the Dutchman Eduard van Beinum. A wide-ranging and cosmopolitan collection of musicians indeed. Like *The Dream of Gerontius*, Elgar's Concerto had survived an under-rehearsed premiere to become one of the most celebrated and widely performed of his works.[1]

Yet as Harrison clearly discerned, there was something extraordinary in the Oxford-born teenager's response to a weary and ageing composer's masterpiece. In 1958, at 13, du Pré had devoured it with a single-mindedness which surprised even her teacher, William Pleeth, who had gently suggested she take it home and look at it. In two days she had memorized the first movement and half of the second; within little more than a year she was performing it at the Royal Albert Hall with the Ernest Read Senior Orchestra, the eponymous Read himself (founder of the renowned series of concerts for children) conducting a group of players which boasted flautists Hilary du Pré—Jacqueline's sister—and a 19-year-old James Galway.

Thus began a 14-year-long relationship. Between that children's concert and her last performance of the work in February 1973 when she was just 28, Jacqueline du Pré was to play it more than any other concerto, although a precise figure is hard to determine. A trawl through the ledgers of her agent Ibbs and Tillett, now held in the library of London's Royal College of Music, reveals a wide range of places and conductors, including three early performances in 1962: with Rudolf Schwarz and the BBC Symphony Orchestra at the Royal Festival Hall, in Chester Cathedral with Sir Adrian Boult and the BBC Northern Symphony Orchestra (nowadays the BBC Philharmonic), and in Stavanger, a 'first' for both the work and its 17-year-old soloist. Other names which crop up include Donald Johanos in Dallas, Stanislav Skrowaczewski in Minneapolis (neither city had previously heard the Concerto), Kurt Adler in Munich, Jascha Horenstein, Charles Groves, Louis Lane in Cleveland, John Pritchard and Norman Del Mar, with whom a BBC recording of a 1962 Royal Festival Hall performance survives. It is a remarkable document, but only half the story compared with what was soon to emerge. One day, no doubt, a zealous researcher burrowing among dusty tapes in some distant radio station's archives will unearth yet another du Pré Elgar Concerto from one of these partnerships, but for the moment it appears that there are eight extant recordings of this instantly recognizable artist in the work which she shaped so memorably in her own image, and which in many ways shaped her. How many artists have provided a wider recorded choice in a single work?

Like many music-obsessed teenagers of the 1960s, I stumbled upon Jacqueline du Pré's Elgar by way of her 1965 EMI studio recording, and was thunderstruck by her playing in the cadenza at the start of the second movement.

The daring double-stopped slide up to the *sforzando* minim, the supercharged high quaver A natural which must surely, I marvelled, threaten the structural integrity of the instrument; no-one previously in this Concerto had conveyed more vividly the turmoil and emotional vulnerability at the heart of Elgar's personality—least of all in the recording studio. Probably more than any other recording, it was this uninhibited 'truth of the heart', in Casals' words, which helped shape my scepticism as a recording producer that 'live' must by definition always be more exciting than 'studio'. Here was an artist to whom the idea of 'marking' in the manner of a rehearsing singer seemed never to have occurred.[2] That famous recording, made in London's Kingsway Hall (long demolished and long missed), was completed in less than a day. 'How could anyone take longer?' she was supposed to have asked her producer. 'In two three-hour sessions you could play the piece twelve times if you were so inclined.' As it was, the session sheets reveal quite a few complete takes of each movement but very few smaller takes for corrections.

How did Jacqueline du Pré do it? Was her playing as purely instinctive as we are led to believe by many of her friends and colleagues? Notwithstanding her apparently ingenuous response to the recording process, things are probably not that simple. Her essential style was certainly free, rhapsodic and unhindered by technical pedantry. A friend who had lessons with her remembers being urged conspiratorially 'not to be afraid of faking something technically if it works'. On the other hand, a glimpse from a filmed lesson she gave a young Moray Welsh combines this characteristic technical unorthodoxy with strongly thought-out and rigorously maintained ideas. Taking Welsh through the 9/8 melody of the first movement, she sings her preferred fingering:

Cellists will recognize this straightaway as encapsulating Jacqueline du Pré's inimitable shaping of the melody: the first-finger slide between the D and E in bar 2, the deliciously 'illegal' moving on the fourth finger at the end of bar 3 and on the first finger for three notes at the beginning of bar 4, the A and D which become harmonics in bars 1 and 3 respectively (though the harmonic D was a variable, as was the 4–2 at the end of bar 4, notes she occasionally played on the D string). Other players might copy this individuality at their peril! It sounds wonderfully spontaneous when she plays it, yet her fingering throughout the Concerto remains almost as unaltered a template in all eight recordings as her characteristic, career-long use of the open A string to convey intensity or 'ache'.[3]

However, while that technical template sounds virtually consistent, Jacqueline du Pré's *musical* personality changes and develops in a way which owes much to two influences above most others: the encroaching illness, unidentified for several years, which was to end her playing career, and the conductors with whom she worked. Two of these affected her artistic development more than any of those listed above: Daniel Barenboim and Sir John Barbirolli—'JB'

to his intimates and colleagues, who conducts the London Symphony Orchestra on the 1965 EMI studio recording. It is a justly renowned performance, a best-seller in the tradition of Dennis Brain's Mozart horn concertos and Mahler's *Das Lied von der Erde* with Kathleen Ferrier. Like these, it has never been out of the catalogue.

Barbirolli's and the young du Pré's paths had crossed nine years earlier when the 11-year-old Jackie won the Suggia Gift, a competition named after Pablo Casals' flamboyant student and sometime lover, Guilhermina Suggia. Barbirolli, talented cellist, great conductor, passionate man and passionate Elgarian (he claimed never to be able to conduct the closing pages of Elgar's Second Symphony, even in rehearsal, without the onset of tears), had sat on the judging panel. He had also played among the orchestral cellists at the Concerto's premiere in 1919. It was inevitable, then, that a bond should be formed. Their first performance of the work together took place at London's Royal Festival Hall on 7 April 1965 with Barbirolli's Hallé Orchestra. No tape survives, but it may be reasonably assumed that the EMI recording of a few months later bears the same hallmarks of this remarkable partnership.[4] In preparation for the sessions, soloist and conductor would apparently talk through the Concerto at piano rehearsals at which the piano would hardly be touched, and it would be a hard heart which resisted du Pré's shaping of the first movement's lilting 9/8 theme or the elegiac manner (notwithstanding the concentration-breaker of a producer's ringing telephone) with which Barbirolli introduces it a few moments earlier on violas and cellos. And yet . . . is it possible to detect perhaps a little too clearly in such affectionately shaped playing the pervasive voice of a benevolent mentor, examining in loving detail with his gifted protégée every note's colour, length and intensity?

In some moods I find myself thinking so. Better this, though, than a preserved invitation concert with Antal Doráti and the BBC Symphony Orchestra at the Corporation's Maida Vale Studios shortly before a USA tour – du Pré's first appearance there – earlier the same year. Hastily dispatched opening solo chords, Dorati's earthbound conducting of the syncopations in the passionate central episode of the slow movement and a feeling of autopilot in much of the *Finale* make it hard to believe that du Pré relished the collaboration. A lighter and more sympathetic grip on the reins from Sir Malcolm Sargent at a 1963 Prom performance (once briefly available on an Italian pirate label) elicits an altogether happier response from her. They had first performed the Concerto together during the previous season, were to do so at the next two, and if Sargent's admiration was not entirely reciprocated (apparently du Pré's nickname for the celebrated if sometimes rather grandiose conductor was 'Mr Snooty-Drawers'), there seems to be no sign of musical incompatibility. Several notches faster than with Barbirolli, the opening 9/8 is sensitive but free-flowing, the slow movement wistful in contrast to the generous outpouring of later performances. Emotional withers are not wrung in that upward double-stopped leap

at which, rather than sliding dramatically between the chords as she usually did, she opts, like Casals in 1945, to hit the high minim out of nowhere (and, rather engagingly, like him, she misses). The second movement is nimble with some beautifully light, prompt accompaniment, the two *Largamente* episodes

declamatory but not hysterical as they sometimes became in later years. For evidence that du Pré's performances were susceptible to the personality on the rostrum, a comparison between this and the 1965 Barbirolli is among the most revealing.

However, it is Barbirolli at a 1967 concert recorded in Prague by the BBC who presents a temperament strikingly different from his 1965 studio self. Whether in concert hall or recording studio, du Pré nearly always sounded 'live', but as a broadcast of Elgar's First Symphony by Barbirolli and the Hallé Orchestra at the 1970 King's

Lynn Festival shows, here was an artist who was often at his most communicative in front of an audience: his 1962 EMI Philharmonia recording of the same symphony, though beautifully played, sounds suave beside the fearless King's Lynn account, given less than five days before his death.[5] So it is with the Prague Elgar Concerto, which opened a BBC Symphony Orchestra tour of Eastern Europe. The first eight bars of the Finale—truculent and much faster than in the studio—make the point in a nutshell. Match that, Barbirolli seems to be challenging his soloist. And, in the manner of a great orator, she does. As a record of the equality of the du Pré/Barbirolli partnership, this is the one to have. The illusion of time suspended at the high *pianissimo* solo D two-thirds of the way through the slow movement is unforgettable. Yet the beautiful details add up structurally: in the sixteen months since the EMI recording, all sense of a conductor at a one-to-one rehearsal guiding his young soloist through every nuance has disappeared. She sometimes leads Barbirolli a merry dance, leaving him behind more than once in the second movement (in which, having set in motion a hair-raising *accelerando* for the coda, she derails herself at the concluding *pizzicatos*). She is clearly having a whale of a time which, given the events of the preceding months and days, is hardly surprising.

Not only had she recently returned from a six-month period of study with Rostropovich in Moscow, but shortly before embarking on the Eastern European tour, the 25-year-old Argentinian-born Israeli Daniel Barenboim had appeared in her life. To this day a conductor and pianist of prolific musical appetite, mental agility and phenomenal memory ('Danny can "photocopy" a score into his brain after reading it once or twice', a conductor colleague has remarked), the effect of his arrival in Jacqueline du Pré's life can hardly be overestimated. The story of their meeting is well known: both had recently recovered from glandular fever and had relished comparing symptoms by phone before meeting at a party at the pianist Fou Ts'ong's house where they had played sonatas together into the small hours. Not only was their relationship and subsequent marriage in Jerusalem after the Six Day War in 1967 a gift to the press (even the tabloids' portrayal of them was as glamorous as many which were lavished on that swinging decade's golden youth of the rock world); theirs was also one of the most remarkable musical partnerships of the twentieth century, as exciting for the temperamental differences between them as for the similarities. For du Pré, the new lifestyle must have had a giddying effect. In many ways the product of the rural English middle class, she now found herself part of an intense world of relentless touring with colleagues of unlimited energy and powerful intellect. From this time until the end of her career, the majority of her performances of the Elgar Concerto were with Barenboim conducting. There are two very different available recordings.

The first, from the year of their marriage, is contained in Christopher Nupen's enthralling and moving film portrait of her and deserves the deep gratitude of all who are fascinated by the sight as well as the sound of a great musician in action. Although I heard Jacqueline du Pré in the flesh only once, part of the key to understanding her approach to music has always seemed to me to lie in the ability to watch her acute response to every note she played. Not everyone feels the same: some find such visible abandon a distraction, although young friends to whom I've played the performance at the heart of this documentary sit mesmerized from first note to last (every patronizing, 'yoof'-obsessed crossover merchant in today's short-span concentration culture should be force-fed this film). Either way, three things are superbly captured by the documentary which precedes the Elgar performance: the headiness of music making among supremely talented friends (the young Itzhak Perlman, Pinchas Zukerman and Zubin Mehta share banter and high seriousness with du Pré and Barenboim), the spirit of a decade in which all things seemed possible, and the depth of rapport between two people who are clearly fascinated by each other. The performance of the Concerto, shot in real time and in black and white, makes a virtue out of its television studio environment, with cameras moving audibly on their tracks. A small audience, including members of the du Pré family, adds to the intimate feeling. Barenboim, scoreless, is captured full-frontally on an unrailed rostrum, while du Pré sits directly in front of him (allowing her to flash him a radiant smile, head upturned, at the end of the second movement). The New Philharmonia Orchestra is spread out panoramically in a way which may seem a little archaic beside the hear-the-note-see-the-note school of today's televised orchestras, but no matter: the spontaneity and euphoria of the solo performance are irresistible, the individuality of fingering and natural technique there for all to see. Her bow bounces with abandon in the last movement: the devil take Elgar's marked slur over these demisemiquavers, she seems to say as she ricochets through them, unslurring, on a powerful, full-length upbow—as much a delight to the eyes as to the ears

The slow movement also offers young cellists a fine chance to observe at close quarters the secret of the du Pré slide (they may also be intrigued to see how often she tucks her little finger *behind* the bow; her sister Hilary has told me that this was because Jacqueline's next finger was unusually long, allowing it to offer more anchorage than her 'pinkie').

Comparison between this and the other recorded account with Barenboim makes for disturbing listening. Hints of the yet undiagnosed multiple sclerosis which was to end her career in 1973 were starting to make themselves felt by the time of this taping, edited from two 1970 concerts with the Philadelphia Orchestra, and while at this stage of the disease it may be unwise to read too much into what one hears on this frequently reissued recording (technically, she is still on top of the work), I must admit to finding it hard to listen to. The most arresting difference between this and all the other recordings we have of du Pré's Elgar is the *sound* of the cello. With the upfront solo balance, it soon becomes clear that the strings are being hit very hard indeed, the bow drawn heavily, resulting in rasping tone and overprojection. Convinced that her Gofriller cello was no longer providing the depth and volume of sound she needed—or perhaps unable to understand why her muscles were beginning to weaken—she had started playing a newly built instrument by Sergio Peresson. Both this recording and that cello have many admirers (to this day Barenboim himself is reported to think well of the instrument), but to my ears an element of hysteria is unmistakable. In the second movement's two *Largamente* episodes

the comma-emphasized semiquaver rests have become lengthened to the point of self-parody—a double-bass player, crashing in half a bar early, clearly cannot believe his ears either—while the A natural in the sixth bar emerges as a lacerating sonic gash.

The continuing popularity of this recording saddens and puzzles me almost as much as the unavailability of Jacqueline du Pré's final two encounters with Elgar's Concerto. Both of them took place in the same week of 1973 (8 and 11 February) at the Royal Festival Hall with Zubin Mehta conducting the New Philharmonia Orchestra, and the first was relayed on Radio 3. That the BBC did not retain the tape is perhaps forgivable in the light of the optimistic tone with which the press promoted the events: billed as part of 'Jacqueline du Pré's return to the concert platform' after a sabbatical full of fear, doubt and bewildering physical symptoms, the return was nevertheless a false dawn. Two weeks later, a disastrous Brahms Double Concerto in New York with Pinchas Zukerman and Leonard Bernstein closed the book on her playing career. The diagnosis of multiple sclerosis was delivered within a fortnight; like the British pianist Solomon, whose stroke in 1956 left him incapacitated for the remaining thirty-two years of his life, she was to enjoy no remission from the disease until her death in October 1987. As so often when a broadcasting organization has wiped an important recording, it is the amateur who comes to the rescue: an off-air taping of the 1973 Elgar survives at the British Library Sound Archive, available to be heard though not to be taken from the building. To listen is to be reminded poignantly of how much the work meant to Jacqueline du Pré. Significant technical blemishes are remarkably few. The weakness of the opening chords makes one fear the worst, yet the C natural in the third bar,

though played softly without the *sforzando* attack Elgar specified, hints wistfully at the shape of many affecting things to come. She takes more time than previously in the slow movement, holding on to phrases as if loath to let them go, and the two lamenting upward slides of a seventh come within a whisker of exaggeration. Indeed, some will judge a line of acceptability to have been crossed, yet the pathos and sincerity are palpable, and the old fire takes hold in the last movement development during the six full-score pages of semiquaver ramblings which here get faster and faster. Or is this perhaps the sound of a woman on the edge of her nerves, suspecting that after these two concerts she will not be returning to this *leitmotiv* of her career? At the end of the semiquavers, she alights on the high F with a palpitating, airy quality which sounds close to relief. Listening alone in a British Library booth, I repeatedly attempted to banish all sentimental inference of du Pré's state of mind. The music is the thing. Then came the *poco piu lento*, the return of the despair which lies at the heart of this Concerto.

Elgar marks these bars *forte molto espressivo*, but here, in 1973, she plays them as a spectral *pianissimo*. The effect is heartbreaking. As a full-circle document of an artist's unique relationship with a work, this recording, obtrusive coughing and all, surely deserves currency.

What would Jacqueline du Pré's Elgar have sounded like today in her sixties? Had not early signs of illness wrought havoc with her state of mind, might we have been spared the hysterical interlude of the 1970 Philadelphia taping? Would there eventually have been some 'paring off' of the emotional abundance that was always a vital part of her personality?[6] Not too much of the latter, I would like to think, whatever new insights maturity would have brought. Daniel Barenboim's pianist compatriot Martha Argerich, whom critics used to accuse of excessive temperament, shows no unwelcome sign of calming down in her sixties, and du Pré's unique response to Elgar's Concerto has inspired two generations of cellists in a way matched by no other interpreter of this work. If, as some say, we have reached an age when artists too often sound the same as, rather than distinct from, each other, then I suspect that we will be treasuring the individuality of a Jacqueline du Pré more than ever in decades to come.

Notes

1 The unfortunate premiere was given by Felix Salmond, another distinguished chamber musician, only three months before Beatrice Harrison's first recording. In later years, reported the pianist Victor Aller, Salmond 'never once referred to the work'. I am indebted to Dr Northrop Moore for this information.

2 The most vivid evidence of this can be heard on du Pré's 1968 EMI recording of Strauss's *Don Quixote*. Sessions at Abbey Road Studios were aborted when Otto Klemperer withdrew at the end of the first day, leaving a Royal Festival Hall performance later in the week without a conductor. Not only did Sir Adrian Boult take over the concert, he and du Pré took the opportunity to rehearse the work at Abbey Road on what would have been the third day of recording. The final rehearsal run-through was captured by a quick-thinking engineer—except that 'run-through' is hardly the word for du Pré's no-holds-barred portrayal of Cervantes' hero. When I discovered and prepared these tapes for release in 1994, I drew on the surviving Klemperer material to drop tiny corrections into the Boult rehearsal footage, and the CD was issued the following year (EMI 5 55528 2). Had du Pré been able in later years to revisit the work in the studio, the result would undoubtedly have had more depth and polish, but here is a moving 'candid' snapshot.

3 How sad that du Pré felt unable to produce an edition of the Concerto during her performing career. By the time she attempted one in the late 1970s, Moray Welsh reports that the characteristic individuality had become destructively interventionist, to the extent of altering many of Elgar's markings of dynamic and expression. The edition fell at the first post.

4 The official reasons for EMI's use of the LSO instead of the Hallé in this recording (the cost of bringing the Manchester players to London and EMI's dislike of the available Manchester venues) have never rung true to me. Barbirolli's celebrated recording of *The Dream of Gerontius* was made in Manchester's Free Trade Hall, while any number of Barbirolli/Hallé projects around this time (including sessions for Delius' *Appalachia*, Elgar's Second Symphony and all seven Sibelius symphonies) took place in London.

5 Issued on BBC Legends BBCL 4106–2, coupled with Elgar's *Introduction and Allegro* from the same concert.

6 'Jackie is sometimes accused of excessive emotion . . . but I love it. When you are young, you should have an excess of everything. If you haven't an excess when you are young, what are you going to pare off as the years go by?' (Sir John Barbirolli in Christopher Nupen's 1967 film).

The Recordings

Jacqueline du Pré/BBC Symphony Orchestra/Norman Del Mar
Royal Festival Hall, London, 24 October 1962
Unissued BBC Recording

Jacqueline du Pré/BBC Symphony Orchestra/Sir Malcolm Sargent
Henry Wood Promenade Concert, Royal Albert Hall, London, 22
   August 1963
(coupled with Elgar's *The Music Makers*, cond. Sargent—concert at
   Royal Albert Hall, 1965)
CD: Intaglio INCD 7351 (pirate issue, nla)

Jacqueline du Pré/BBC Symphony Orchestra/Antal Dorati
Invitation Concert, BBC Studios, Maida Vale, London, 3 April
   1965
Unissued BBC Recording

Jacqueline du Pré/London Symphony Orchestra/Sir John Barbirolli
Kingsway Hall, London, 19 August 1965
CD: EMI 'Great Recordings of the Century' 5 62886–2
(coupled with Elgar's *Sea Pictures* (Janet Baker/LSO/Barbirolli)/
   Overture: *Cockaigne* (Philharmonia/Barbirolli))

Jacqueline du Pré/BBC Symphony Orchestra/Sir John Barbirolli
Shetartum Hall, Prague, 3 January 1967
CD: Testament SBT 1388
(coupled with Bach's Cello Suites 1 & 2—BBC studio recordings,
   1962) A short clip from those artists' performance in the Grand
   Hall of Moscow Conservatorie was filmed by a Soviet news crew,
   and can be seen on the DVD below.

Jacqueline du Pré/New Philharmonia Orchestra/Daniel Baren-
   boim
BBC Wood Lane Studios, London, 1967
Contained in 'Jacqueline du Pré in Portrait'. A film by Christopher
   Nupen.

DVD: Opus Arte/Allegro Films OA CN0902 D

Jacqueline du Pré/Philadelphia Orchestra/Daniel Barenboim

Edited from concerts at the Academy of Music, Philadelphia, 27 & 28 November 1970

CD: Sony SB2K 63247 (2 CD set coupled with *Enigma Variations/* Overture: *Cockaigne* (Ormandy); *Pomp and Circumstance* Marches (Andrew Davis); Violin Concerto (Zukerman/Barenboim))

Jacqueline du Pré/New Philharmonia Orchestra/Zubin Mehta

Royal Festival Hall, London, 8 February 1973

Unissued BBC Recording. Off-air copy available to hear at the British Library Sound Archive, London.

Shelf mark: 1CDR0022825.

Listening appointments: 020 7412 7418.

(A Readers' Ticket, bookable in advance, is necessary to gain admission.)

Part 4: The Legacy

15

An Honoured Trust: The Elgar Foundation and the Birthplace Museum

MICHAEL MESSENGER

The visitor to Broadheath may well wonder why Elgar is celebrated in a modest, rather cramped country cottage, three miles from Worcester, rather than in one of the grander houses he occupied during his later years of fame. The truth is that, even though he spent only the first two years of his life there, Edward Elgar retained a deep sentimental attachment to the cottage in which he was born and, late in life, actually said to his friend and fellow-composer Herbert Howells, 'I don't expect much from the nation, but if ever they think it worthwhile, I wish they would buy this little cottage. It's the only wish I've got, about the nation and me.'[1]

In the absence of any action by the government of the day, that challenge was taken up by his daughter, Carice Elgar Blake, shortly after her father's death in 1934, and she immediately began negotiations to buy the cottage (then called 'The Firs'). Worcester Corporation, however, wished to commemorate its most famous son and, after considering various alternatives and taking soundings from Sir Ivor Atkins, who advised the Council that Sir Edward would have liked the cottage to be acquired, and learning that Carice was prepared to transfer her interest to them, determined on its purchase for the sum of £400 plus legal fees.[2] Following completion in May 1935,[3] the Corporation agreed to lease it at a peppercorn rent to the trust that Carice herself created: the Elgar Birthplace Trust.[4] An appeal was launched under the chairmanship of Sir Landon Ronald, with the intention of creating an endowment fund capable of providing the £250 per annum it was then thought necessary to maintain the Birthplace and its collections.[5]

This received the active support of the *Daily Telegraph*, which itself donated 100 guineas and published lengthy lists of donors, ranging from an anonymous gift of 6d. and 'a widow's mite' of one shilling (about five pence of present currency) to the £50 from Baron Frédéric d'Erlanger (now barely remembered as a composer, although his opera based on Hardy's *Tess of the D'Urbervilles* had been produced at Covent Garden many years earlier), and a number of lesser, though still substantial, contributions such as the £20 from Yehudi Menuhin. By mid-November 1935, over £3,000 had been raised, but it was not only money that was being given: Troyte Griffith and Dora Powell (the 'Troyte' and 'Dorabella' of Elgar's *Enigma Variations*) each provided a rose tree for the garden,[6] while the former also offered some of his souvenirs to the new museum.[7]

Carice herself seems to have been assiduous in contacting friends and acquaintances and collected a substantial amount of material which, even today, forms the core of the collection, though there have been any number of significant additions through gift, bequest and purchase in the intervening years. Today, it comprises a vast number of letters, manuscript and printed scores, family scrap-books, programmes, pictures, photographs, and other memora-bilia, and offers a rich source for the many research workers who visit the Birthplace; but despite this it still receives no direct government funding.

It both is and is not a 'shrine' in the traditional sense of the word. It is, in that there remains an almost indefinable sense of magic in this place, though the ghost of Elgar walks but occasionally through the tiny rooms; Dame Janet Baker, an eminent interpreter of Elgar's music, has written movingly of the sense of place[8] and the whole building is permeated by the man—his life, his family, his character, his many enthusiasms—and in that sense, it certainly is a shrine, a place of pilgrimage. The contrary argument, though, is that although the garden retains a superficial similarity to that portrayed in J. C. Buckler's well-known study of 1856, within the cottage walls no attempt has been made to recreate the precise state and atmosphere of the building during the brief period when the Elgars lived there, even were that known. It has always been a working museum wherein the composer's interests have been displayed, and even the study, which Carice laboured over in the 1930s, was an attempt to re-establish the study from Elgar's Hereford home of the first decade of the twentieth century.[9] There is, too, the issue of the 'birthroom', now simply part of the large upstairs landing following the decision in 1989 to remove the partition walls[10] (subsequently stated to have been erected in 1946[11]); this certainly facilitated circulation and display, but seems curiously alien in concept to modern notions of privacy and decorum. The Elgars would not have been the first family of modest means to have relied upon screens and curtaining, but Edward Elgar on his visit with Howells certainly implied a separate room; even if this were the case was its size and location precisely that of the later addition? There can be no certainty beyond that 'The Firs' of 1935 when Carice assumed control differed, at least in detail, from the same building in 1857.

1935 was Worcester's turn to host the annual Three Choirs Festival, and in September Carice invited a few of her father's friends and colleagues to visit the Birthplace; these included W. H. ('Billy') Reed, Gerald Finzi, Arnold Bax and Ralph Vaughan Williams.[12] However, it was not until the next Three Choirs Festival in Worcester in September 1938 that Carice, after a period of intensive preparation, was able to realize her ambition and open the museum more generally, every day during the Festival itself but thereafter reverting to a part-time basis. The fact that it could open at all in the absence of a responsible curator/caretaker was due to her having moved, with her husband Samuel Blake, from Surrey to Broadheath into a small house, 'Woodend', only a stone's throw from Elgar's birthplace. The need for her constant presence was obviated in 1939 by the appointment of a 'curator' who, with her husband, lived on the premises, occupying as much as half of the building and remaining in post until her death in 1964. Clearly there was little space to display the material that had been collected, with, for example, only a representative selection of Elgar's extensive personal library being retained, and it could only be a matter of time before the situation became untenable.

Records from this period are scanty. The Birthplace Trust had held its inaugural formal meeting on 20 October 1936, chaired by Sir Landon Ronald and with just four of the five trustees present,[13] but there appear to be no further extant minutes until the mid-1950s; it would be surprising if no further meetings were held during the first few years, if only to review the financial situation, but in reality it is almost certain (and this can be deduced from the few brief entries in Carice's diary that concern the museum) that decisions affecting its operation and collections were taken by Carice herself.

The museum remained open during the war years, still on a part-time basis, and indeed the very few visitors it received justified nothing more; but with the return of peace, thoughts could once again turn to developing the museum. Restricted space, the fact that the cottage still served as the home of the curator with the front door opening directly into her living room, and the fear of spoiling the atmosphere that pervaded house and garden meant that little could be done there, but with the help of her friend Sybil Russell, Carice did open a tearoom in her own garden at 'Woodend', using a temporary structure and fitting it out.[14] It was not until the purchase by the Foundation of the adjacent Rose Cottage in 1979 that the curator was able to vacate the Birthplace and the displays could be expanded.

The contribution of successive curators and the numerous changes to the trustees are carefully chronicled elsewhere,[15] as are the recollections of those visiting the Birthplace; but a key factor in its future development was the post-war resurgence of interest in Elgar's music and the resultant growth in Elgar scholarship. The role of the Birthplace as a vital source of information, and perhaps even inspiration, was increasingly recognized, though that in itself created additional pressures. In those seemingly halcyon days family scrapbooks and diaries, as well as many mementos of Elgar's life and career, were left on open shelves, unsupervised for much of the time, and such trust was widely respected.

By 1955, the trust fund stood at a little over £3,600 and, with an annual income of £170 and the curator paid no more than £2 a week, the situation was relatively stable. There was a realization that, with the facilities in the cottage as poor as they were, there needed to be improved, preferably separate, accommodation for the curator. Initial attempts to persuade Worcester City Council to buy an adjacent plot of land for this purpose eventually foundered, and the Trustees considered instead an extension involving the development of the linked stable block. The plans for this were finally approved in 1966, but before it could be achieved the Trust needed to raise an additional £10,000, and a fund-raiser (Bernard van Dieren) was appointed. Within a year the target figure had risen to £25,000, and Van Dieren and Carice Elgar Blake set about raising the money with the latter's customary determination, including a tour to the USA which, however, failed in its main purpose.

In 1970 Carice Elgar Blake died, leaving to the 'Trustees of the Elgar Birthplace all manuscripts scores and other papers now or hereafter kept or lodged at the Birthplace including the Second Symphony'.[16] She had left the area for North Somerset some years earlier, claiming that Worcester was not what it had been,[17] but her commitment to the Birthplace never flagged. In a real sense it remains her creation and a living testimony, not only to the genius of her father but also to her unwavering dedication and determination, and in 2001 the directors of the Foundation recognized this by naming the new recital-lecture room in the Centre after her.

With her passing came a new era. Van Dieren was not long to survive, and after initially backing his ambitious plans for establishing an all-embracing national organization focusing on Elgar and thus helping to ensure a secure future for the Birthplace, the Trustees bowed to political pressure, and he was forced to resign. Andrew Neill has argued persuasively that Van Dieren's sins were of incompetence rather than veniality, that his attempt to create a 'United Kingdom Elgar Society', while failing to consider the autonomous Elgar Society (which had been established in 1951), even to the extent of involving the Prime Minister of the day, Edward Heath, was both tactless and ill-considered rather than a measured insult, and that the haemorrhaging of Trust money, another claim made against him at the time, was poor financial management and nothing worse.[18] Nearly forty years later a

similarly ambitious scheme, this time to create an umbrella organization embracing the Elgar Foundation (which had subsumed the
Trust), the Society and the Elgar family was to founder, largely
because of the different aims and management of the former two
elements; but by that time the need was perceived as less acute since
all those involved were cooperating in a number of different ways,
with the Society acting as a virtual 'Friends of the Museum', having
agreed in 2001 to make an annual donation to the museum, and the
Elgar family, both acting individually and through the Will Trust,
proving generous benefactors.

Following the departure of Van Dieren in 1971, the parlous state
of the Trust's finances needed to be rectified with several of the
Trustees themselves being forced to contribute money from their
personal resources, and a major appeal, with a dedicated fund-
raiser and committees in London and the West Midlands, was
launched in 1975, initially to put the Foundation's finances on an
altogether sounder footing. The Birthplace Trust had but limited
powers, another factor in Van Dieren's thinking perhaps, and some
two years earlier in 1973 the Elgar Foundation had been created,
with the same membership as the Trust but with the ability to own
land, trade and undertake a range of activities wider than those
directly involved with the Birthplace cottage; over the years it has,
for example, raised money for the Elgar statue in Worcester,
commissioned new works for the Three Choirs Festival and
awarded an annual scholarship to a Worcester Cathedral chorister,
but its main focus was, and remains, the Elgar Birthplace
Museum.

The inadequacy of the Birthplace cottage remained, and the next
twenty years is a story of the struggle to create an acceptable
solution to the problem. It was partly alleviated with the purchase
of Rose Cottage in 1979, but the Trustees recognized that if the
ambitions of Elgar's daughter and her successor Trustees to create
a worthy centre for Elgarian scholarship and understanding were to
be realized, further expansion was necessary. The creation in 1990
of a secure, environmentally controlled room for the display of
manuscripts was a demonstration of intent, but public display
space was still horribly cramped and facilities for researchers were
pitiful.

The Trustees had had second thoughts about a sizeable extension to the cottage, and instead proposed building on land between the cottage and a neighbouring bungalow, 'The Elms', which had been purchased in 1988.[19] Following a series of cogent and publicly voiced objections to the size of the proposed building and its propinquity to the Birthplace cottage, it was agreed to demolish 'The Elms', lower the height of the new Centre and locate it further away behind the cottage, but the way to achieve this was not finally cleared until 1992, when the Foundation was able to buy some land to the rear of the cottage.[20] A major development appeal had been launched in 1990 and had generated enough money for a start to be made upon the proposed new visitor centre, designed, following the expressed wishes of the Foundation's Patron, HRH The Prince of Wales, using the concept of a traditional Worcestershire barn, set in a landscaped area planted with traditional Worcestershire and Herefordshire varieties of apple and pear bought with money raised as part of the appeal.

Building work began in 1994 and, though resources were insufficient to complete the building, optimism ran high that, with the shell in place, the necessary funds would soon be donated. Thoughts turned to the National Lottery, which had just been launched, and the Trustees saw the opportunity to achieve their ambition sooner than might otherwise have been the case and an application was submitted later that year. It was, alas, ill-conceived with no professional curatorial input and a resultant lack of clarity in the relationship between the two buildings and, even more critically, attendance figures that were wildly optimistic, postulating as many as 30,000 visitors a year, significantly more than the number that the Birthplace cottage itself could physically have accommodated. It was rejected.

It was evident that far greater professionalism was necessary before any further progress could be made, with the initial step being the first ever appointment of a qualified museum curator. This in turn led to changes within the operation of the museum and its eventual award by the Museums Association (in 1997) of the much-coveted Registered Museum status. The thoughts of the Foundation Board, though, were never far from the problem of completing the shell of the Centre which had by now lain empty since 1995, was looking understandably neglected and was widely regarded as a reproach to the Foundation, but the Trustees had already resolved to attempt the lottery route once more.

Nearly two years of preparation followed. Initial discussions with lottery officers revealed that the guidelines were being redrawn, but even after these were published some months later the application could not be drafted. The Heritage Lottery Fund, apparently disturbed by the precarious existence of some of the capital schemes it had funded in the past, had shifted its focus to collection care and management, and the Foundation first needed to establish that capital costs necessary for the proper care and display of the material (including the completion of the raw shell that was the Centre itself) could be included. And there was one important addition to the Foundation's plans: the inclusion of enhanced strongroom and research facilities for its unique holdings, and this within the curtilage of the cottage itself by extending into the stable block while retaining the external appearance of the building. This was to prove crucial in the future development of the collection.

The Chairman of the Management Committee and professional Museum staff held a number of meetings with lottery officers in London, Broadheath and Worcester seeking advice and clarification and it was August 1999 before the completed submission, comprising four volumes and measuring three inches thick, could be sent. The curatorial input from the Birthplace's own staff was now substantial and the distinction between the two buildings was more sharply drawn, with the public displays within the cottage focussing upon Elgar the man—his background, his many interests, his travels—while those within the Centre, with its environmentally controlled cases, were primarily concerned with his music.

There was a last-minute intervention by Worcestershire County Council seeking space for its dispersed Music and Arts Unit, and the Foundation adjusted its plans to accommodate this, realizing that the additional revenue from rent and a share of the running costs would help to ensure financial viability. The revised submission was agreed by the Heritage Lottery Fund, which provided support of just over 60%, tenders were sought, designers agreed, and work begun.[21] The amount of space let to the County Council necessitated imaginative use of the remaining central area, now extended outwards to incorporate a reception area and a greatly expanded shop, incorporating a privately commissioned painting of the 'Enigma Variations' by internationally known artist Norman Perryman, who specialized in musical subjects and many of whose paintings are displayed in Birmingham's Symphony Hall. The solution adopted for the displays was to create an inner 'drum' from which much natural light could be excluded, so permitting sensitive items to be exhibited in the environmentally controlled cases. At the same time, the outer 'skin', which incorporated some audio features, could be used to display more robust material. The enlarged museum, now operating on a split site with all the difficulties that involved, and for the first time open to the public every day of the week for eleven months of the year, opened its doors to the public in August 2000, with the official ceremony, led by Dame Janet Baker, the Foundation's joint (and subsequently sole) President, held two months later on 19 October.

Following the appointment of a documentation officer, the first in the museum's history, the research room was made available to the public a year later. The collection, which already boasted the manuscript scores of the Second Symphony and the Violin Sonata, had been significantly enhanced with an important donation by the Foundation's other joint president, Wulstan Atkins. He had joined the Foundation in 1973, though his association with Edward Elgar dated back to his boyhood days in Worcester, and his towering and decisive presence on the Board as Trustee, Chairman and finally as an active joint President until his death in 2003, had been a major factor in the Foundation's thinking and actions. His gift of manuscript scores and sketches, including both *Wand of Youth* suites and the *Pomp and Circumstance March* no. 3, as well as some proof scores, originally belonging to Elgar's great friend Ivor Atkins, was a major demonstration of his commitment to the Birthplace, and, in recognition of the significance of this material, the small back room in the cottage was named after the family with some material relating to it and its connection with Edward Elgar invariably displayed there.

The next step was to reclaim the nearly 10,000 letters that had previously been lodged in the local record office, and this was followed by the transfer of a further deposit, this one by the Grafton family, a member of which now represented Elgar's descendants on the Foundation's board, a valuable demonstration of the support now being provided by the Elgar family. It was clear that not only had stringent standards of physical care to be implemented (they were), but also that unsupervised access to what was now a veritable treasure trove of Elgar-related material could not be permitted and that the whole collection needed to be properly documented—a Herculean task since existing records of material accumulated over seventy years were, to say the least, sketchy. The choice of a suitable computer system was not entirely straightforward since it needed to be capable of accommodating printed material, manuscripts and three-dimensional artefacts, and, of course, to be readily accessible by staff and research workers alike; but one was eventually selected and a start made on reducing the backlog of seven decades. The next phase is the digitization of key parts of the archive so that information concerning the museum's holdings is made available worldwide through the Internet.

Material had continued to be received over the years, including, from local sources, the manuscripts of *Froissart*, *The Light of Life* and some of the music composed by Elgar for the Asylum at Powick. The increased strength of its holdings and the growth in use of the research facilities encouraged the Foundation to enter the marketplace and purchase, mostly at auction, a number of important items, including the manuscript scores of *The Severn Suite* (Elgar's only work for brass band), the violin and piano version of *Salut d'amour*, and the composer's musical joke, the so-called 'Smoking Cantata', as well as significant collections of letters to Ernest Newman, C. H. Buck and John Austin. None of this would have been possible without grant aid and, more importantly, the generous help of a few private individuals, most notably the then Chairman David Bowerman and members of the Elgar family. Such activity, though, tended to encourage further gifts, few more important than the items donated by the descendants of Émile Cammaerts who had provided texts for three of Elgar's

World War I pieces supporting the Belgians, though individual objects such as photographs and programmes continue to be added.

The latter is worth special mention, perhaps, as the Elgar Birthplace is rare amongst composer museums in continuing to add some contemporary programmes featuring Elgar's music to its collection, which now numbers several thousand, believing that it is important to chart the continuing popularity of Elgar's music, especially with the centenaries of major works now falling thick and fast. The original programmes for these form part of the collection, as well as others originally gathered by the Elgars themselves, with one of the earliest dating from 12 June 1840, recording a recital at Buckingham Palace in which Queen Victoria and Prince Albert together with members of the Court sang with such operatic luminaries as Mario, Lablache and Costa, and possibly retained by Edward's piano-tuner father.

Neither would the continuing enhancement of visitor facilities have been possible without the generosity of a number of benefactors with, for example, the introductory video compiled and donated by a member of the Elgar Society, a successful audio tour narrated by the well-known actor, Gabriel Wolff, with an introduction by Dame Janet Baker, funded by a former Trustee, and an interactive unit containing over 1,300 entries enabling visitors to explore further Elgar's life and work financed from a major legacy.

The attempt by the Foundation to achieve designation for the museum and its archive as a collection of national significance was thwarted in 2004, one hopes only temporarily, but thus restricting the opportunities for enhanced grant funding, and the dependence of the Elgar Birthplace Museum on its own endeavours, backed by private funding, is marked. It certainly throws into sharp relief the absence, to date at least, of direct governmental funding for this important national asset. Clearly, Elgar was right not to expect much of the nation, but with the aid of its many friends the Foundation is attempting to create a stable base and establish the endowment fund that will secure for posterity this important part of Britain's traditional heritage.

Notes

1 Palmer, C., *Herbert Howells—a Centenary Celebration*, 1992, p. 360.
2 Corporation of Worcester Council minutes, 1 January 1935.
3 Worcestershire County Record Office BA.5557: r926:11.
4 Supplemental Declaration of Trust, 1 July 1955, confirming the date of the original Trust Deed as 4 August 1936.
5 *Daily Telegraph*, 29 August 1935.
6 Powell, Mrs R., *Edward Elgar: Memories of a Variation* (London: Oxford University Press, 1937; reprinted 1979), p. 128.
7 Letter from Sir Landon Ronald to A. Troyte Griffith, 17 September 1935 (Manchester Archives and Local Studies, Manchester City Library).
8 Baker, Dame Janet, Foreword in Neill, A., *'It's the only wish I've got . . . ': The Story of the Elgar Birthplace*, 2006.
9 Diary of Carice Elgar Blake, 9 October 1939.
10 Elgar Foundation Finance & General Purposes Sub-Committee minutes, 23 November 1989.
11 Elgar Foundation minutes, 12 January 1993.
12 Elgar Birthplace visitors' book.
13 Trustees of the Elgar Birthplace Fund minutes, 20 October 1936.
14 Wohfeld, H. S., 'Carice Irene Blake: Memories, 1941–1970', *Elgar Society Journal*, Vol. 6 no. 5, May 1990, p. 8.
15 Neill, A., *'It's the only wish I've got . . . ': The Story of the Elgar Birthplace*, 2006.
16 Last Will and Testament of Carice Elgar Blake, 20 December 1968.
17 Carice Elgar Blake to Margaret Nicholl, 25 August 1958 (Malvern Concert Club archive (at the Elgar Birthplace)).
18 Neill, A., *'It's the only wish I've got . . . ': The Story of the Eglar Birthplace*, 2006, pp. 36–40.
19 Elgar Foundation Finance Committee minutes, 6 October 1988.
20 Elgar Foundation Finance & General Purposes Committee minutes, 30 July 1992.
21 *Elgar Society Newsletter* no. 10, March 2000, pp. 17–21.

Index